Prussia

A Captivating Guide to the History of Prussia and Franco-Prussian War

Free Bonus from Captivating History
(Available for a Limited time)

Hi History Lovers!

Now you have a chance to join our exclusive history list so you can get your first history ebook for free as well as discounts and a potential to get more history books for free! Simply visit the link below to join.

Captivatinghistory.com/ebook

Also, make sure to follow us on Facebook, Twitter and Youtube by searching for Captivating History.

Contents

Part 1: History of Prussia

A Captivating Guide to the Kingdom of Prussia and Its Role in the Napoleonic Wars, Franco-Prussian War, and Unification of Germany in 1871

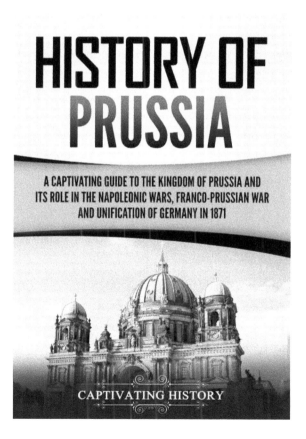

Introduction

Prussia's story, from its inception to its glorious victory through the unification of Germany, is one of an underdog rising to greatness. Over the centuries, the Hohenzollern dynasty led its people and lands, navigating through an obstacle course it seemed destined to fail. Yet, somehow, the Hohenzollerns managed to overcome it, standing atop many other competitors. As such, it can be seen almost as a fairytale or a motivational moral fable. In part, it is exactly that, as Prussia's story follows the classic tale of a small guy who makes it in the world (or, in this case, a small country in a mishmash of medieval German states to a nation-building European power in the late 19th century).

However, at the same time, Prussian history is one marked by militarism, expansionism, and nationalism. Such a portrayal depicts the Prussians as warmongers or a nation of vicious soldiers lacking any scruples. It is seen as a land of "iron and blood." That representation has the same weight and truth to it as the previous, more heroic image. The two are different sides of the same coin, depending solely on our perspective.

This guide will attempt to avoid any judgment of Prussia, regardless of its positive or negative aspects. It will merely retell its story, as it is one that made a substantial mark on European and world history, making it worthy of our attention. It also represents an insight into both German history and culture, as many things that are seen as "quintessentially German" had their roots in Prussia. As such, understanding modern Germany has to be done through the prism of its Prussian ancestors, as they played a key role in the evolution and development of both the German nation and state.

In the end, the Prussian story is one of highs and lows, a meandering tale spanning a long period, showcasing the complexity of the human past. There are wars with victories and losses. There are economic developments and industrialization, educational and religious reforms, diplomacy, trade, and much more. This guide will try to bring you closer to understanding Prussia, Germany, and the history of humankind in general.

Chapter 1 – Humble Origins

Most books concerning Prussian history tend to begin in the 17th century, ignoring centuries of events that helped shaped the development of what was to become the Kingdom of Prussia. With that in mind, this guide will track as far back as possible to set a reference frame in hopes of better understanding the Prussian story.

First, it is important to understand that three components built the Prussian state. The first two are the territories of Brandenburg and Prussia, while the third and most vital is the Hohenzollern dynasty. It emerged from the obscurity of the Middle Ages in the 11th century, with sources mentioning Burkhard I, Count of Zollern, who was the ruler of an estate located in the Swabian Alps. It's most likely that the dynasty got its name from this early title, as in those early days, its members were known only as Zollern. Another possibility is that the name was derived from the castle that was the center of their county rule, but in the end, its name remains somewhat uncertain. Similarly, it is quite likely that Burkhard's ancestors were also part of the nobility, although no credible links or sources confirm that. Thus, he remains crowned as the dynasty's founder.

Later paintings of the first Hohenzollern rulers: Burkhard I (top) and Friedrich I (bottom). Source: https://commons.wikimedia.org

Burkhard's successors slowly increased their possessions, mostly by being loyal subjects of the Holy Roman emperors, yet they remained relatively of low prominence and importance. The first step toward a greater fate was made by Friedrich (Frederick) III, who married the heiress of the Burgraviate of Nuremberg. By 1191, he inherited the territory through his wife and became known as Friedrich I, Burgrave of Nuremberg, as this territory was deemed more reputable and richer due to its developed trade.

It seems that at roughly this time, he renamed his dynasty into the Hohenzollerns, roughly translated as the greater Zollerns, most likely to mark its rise in importance. Upon his death, most likely around 1204, his sons, Conrad and Friedrich, divided the inheritance in half. Since Conrad was older, he was given Zollern, while Friedrich received Nuremberg. However, around 1218, for some unknown reason, the two brothers reshuffled the inheritance and switched titles. With that, the House of Hohenzollern was divided into two branches. The younger Friedrich's branch became known as Swabian, while the older Conrad's line became known as Franconian since Nuremberg was located in the region of Franconia, modern-day northwestern Bavaria.

For the next roughly two hundred years, Conrad and his successors remained rather loyal and dependable allies of the Holy Roman Empire. During that period, through clever politics, they managed to slightly enlarge their possessions around Nuremberg, while the city itself became an unofficial capital of the empire where the Imperial Diet would meet from time to time. However, it was only in the early 15th century that the Hohenzollerns made their next step toward prominence. Around 1410, Frederick (Friedrich) VI gained control of the Margravate of Brandenburg, located in northeastern Germany around the city of Berlin. After initial troubles with subduing the local nobles, Frederick consolidated his control. Then, around 1415, he was officially recognized as its legitimate ruler when he paid 400,000 gold pieces to King

Sigismund of Hungary, who legally owned the title. Thus, he became known as Frederick I, Margrave of Brandenburg, a title hierarchically between a count and a duke.

The lands themselves were relatively unimposing and worthless. Despite being located in the Central European Plain, its soil wasn't very suitable for agriculture, as it was often sandy and of poor quality. It was also filled with marshes and bogs. Brandenburg also lacked any notable mineral or metal deposits. It was linked with the Baltic coast through the Oder and Elbe Rivers, but those were somewhat sluggish and not interconnected waterways. Furthermore, as the area had little to offer trade-wise, a connection to the sea meant little. Additionally, Brandenburg lacked any natural borders, meaning it was open for invasions.

Overall, the region was utterly unimpressive in terms of its material worth. Its true potential lay in its political importance, as the margrave of Brandenburg was one of seven electoral princes of the Holy Roman Empire. Their official task was to designate the next emperor when needed, and as such, it was a rather distinguished title to hold. Thus, Frederick was also known as the elector of Brandenburg (the prince-elector was a separate title from margrave).

A 15ᵗʰ-century portrait of Frederick I, Elector of Brandenburg. Source: https://commons.wikimedia.org

To understand both the importance of such a distinction and the rest of Hohenzollern and Prussian history, one has to know how the Holy Roman Empire functioned. Unlike most other empires, this wasn't as centralized and unified. It was more akin to a loose federation of some three hundred smaller sovereign territorial entities, whose legal relations and status within the empire varied. Furthermore, the imperial title was elective, making its acquisition a proper game of political intrigue. It is also important to note that despite the existence of an Imperial Diet, there wasn't an imperial central government, the right of taxation, or a standing imperial army. Thus, actual imperial power was somewhat limited. Oftentimes, the strength of the ruler depended solely on his personal possessions, skills, connections, and politics, enabling him to gather or force the support of his numerous subjects. Nevertheless, theoretically, the title was still quite prestigious since the Holy Roman Empire was deemed to be the successor of the Roman Empire. In that political landscape, being one of the prince-electors meant having much more influence and a useful diplomatic tool, allowing for trading votes for other types of concessions like territorial gains.

The Hohenzollerns managed to use their newly acquired influence to secure small but important territorial gains throughout the rest of the 15th and early 16th centuries. They traded their support and votes, but despite that, the dynasty remained relatively weak economically and militarily. At roughly the same time, the famous Habsburg dynasty, whose center of power was in Austria, rose up to dominate the Holy Roman Empire. After decades of political instability, in 1452, Habsburgian Frederick III became the emperor. By then, his dynasty held substantial territories across Europe, allowing him and his successors to dominate relatively small imperial states and entities. Thus, from then on, the imperial title factually became hereditary within the Habsburg line, but it officially and theoretically remained elective. The Habsburgs also began reforming the empire, though they never succeeded in centralizing their rule over those lands as they had in their other possessions like Hungary or Bohemia. Additionally, from 1512, the empire was officially named the Holy Roman Empire of the German Nation, despite having subjects of various other ethnicities. Some see this as the birth of an overarching German national identity, though it was still far from how we perceive such things today.

For the Hohenzollerns, this period was also a time of dynastic consolidation. Up to the late 15th century, the family followed a rather common medieval succession tradition of partitioning the estate between brothers. Such a practice allowed for the suitable security of all the ruler's children, which was rooted in the common familial need to take care of one's offspring. However, it was quite counterproductive from a state-building perspective. This led Albert (Albrecht) III Achilles, who succeeded the margravate from his older brother, to pass the Dispositio Achillea in 1473, a law stipulating that Brandenburg must remain whole and could only be solely inherited by his eldest son. However, the rest of the Nurembergian lands remained dividable.

This was the first Hohenzollern succession law, yet it initially was meant to regulate only the matter of Albert's heirs. This notion of an indivisible Brandenburgian estate was confirmed once again in 1541 with the House Treaty of Regensburg, which concerned the redistribution of Nuremberg territories among the later Hohenzollerns. Along the way, there were attempts and even short-term divisions of Brandenburg; however, by the late 16th century, the idea of its unitary nature prevailed among the dynasty, signaling the transformation from clan chiefs into heads of states.

Despite that, the turn of the century proved to be turbulent for the Hohenzollerns, as well as the entire Holy Roman Empire. In 1517, Martin Luther's *Nighty-five Theses* sparked the start of the religious Reformation that formalized the split of Catholics and Protestants. This caused shockwaves across Europe and created numerous religious conflicts, but it proved particularly harmful for the empire's peace. Many of the northern Germanic states turned toward Protestantism, most notably Lutheranism. For the Catholic south, that was heresy, especially for the deeply devoted Habsburgs, who often saw themselves as the bulwarks of Christianity due to the long-lasting clashes with the Ottoman Turks in the Balkans. As such, Emperor Charles V of House Habsburg saw fit to fight against the Lutheran north, also using it to consolidate his imperial rule. With that, the Hohenzollerns found themselves in the midst of the ensuing chaos.

The Swabian line remained Catholic, as did most of the southern Germanic states. However, Brandenburg was heavily influenced by the new religion. When Lutheranism emerged, Prince-elector Joachim I acted like a devoted Catholic, trying to repress it. This was partially because he substantially profited from the selling of indulgences (Martin Luther's biggest issue with the corrupt Catholic Church), which was done by his own brother Albert, who was the archbishop of Magdeburg. In fact, Albert was one of the clerical leaders that sparked Luther's rebellion and one of the people directly accused in the *Nighty-five Theses*. However, his wife, Elizabeth of Denmark, publicly converted to Lutheranism, sparking a split between them.

Along with that, the Brandenburgian commoners began turning toward the new Christian branch, prompting Joachim to force his son and heir Joachim II to sign a contract promising to remain a Catholic. Joachim II honored the agreement but only for a while. By 1539, four years after his father's death and his own ascension to the throne, he converted to Lutheranism. Nevertheless, he refused to force his subjects to follow him while also avoiding any public support for his new religion. Joachim II was worried, quite rightfully, that any excess in such matters might put him and Brandenburg in danger, as the empire was still overwhelmingly Catholic.

Thus, politically, he remained a loyal subject of the Habsburgian emperor. Joachim II even sent a small contingent of troops to aid the emperor in the Schmalkaldic War (1546–1547), a religious conflict with German Lutheran princes. In most cases, Joachim II tried to separate himself from most of the radical and belligerent Lutheran leaders while also refusing to abandon his beliefs. Instead, he tried to secure peace for his realm by attempting to act as a mediator between the two sides. The situation subsided a bit in the 1550s when Holy Roman Emperor Charles V agreed to negotiate with the Protestants. He was partially forced to do this since France began to aid the rebellious princes, seeking to destabilize his reign.

caught Joachim's eyes due to the fact that it was ruled by his cousin from the Hohenzollern side branch, Duke Albert of Prussia.

Albert, the grandson of Albert III Achilles, came to hold that title more by luck than design. As a member of a side branch and a third son, he was poised for a clerical career. He was a devout Catholic and seemed to be a reliable and learned man. Thus, when the Teutonic Order needed a new grandmaster, he was elected for the role in 1511. At the time, the order held Prussia, as it had been present there since the early 13th-century Prussian crusade sought to Christianize the local population. After their goal was achieved, the knights stayed, becoming a rival for surrounding states, most notably Poland and Lithuania. From the mid-15th century, the Teutonic Order saved itself from destruction by accepting suzerainty from Polish kings, becoming a Polish fiefdom. Nevertheless, relations remained strained. In fact, part of the reason why Albert was chosen was due to the fact his mother hailed from the Polish ruling family, making him the king's nephew. Despite his attempts to salvage the situation, he found affairs in Prussia slipping out of his hands. That was when he met with Martin Luther, who persuaded him to adopt Lutheranism and convert Prussia to his personal estate.

1466

A map of Prussia under the Teutonic Knights (in orange). Source:
https://commons.wikimedia.org

Using his ties with the Polish king, Albert managed to secure that. Thus, in 1525, the Duchy of Prussia was formally established, remaining a Polish fiefdom. Simultaneously, Prussia and Albert became among the earliest public supporters of Lutheranism. However, years passed, and as he was nearing the end of his life, he left only a single male heir, Albert Frederick, who was underaged. This prompted Joachim II to act, and in 1564, he used his wife's connections to secure a decree deeming his sons as secondary heirs to the duchy if Albert Frederick died without an heir. This was confirmed four years later when the old duke died.

It was a long-term plan that eventually paid off. Though Albert Frederick lived a long life, dying only in 1618, he left no heirs, as he was mentally ill. However, even before his death, the Brandenburgian Hohenzollerns acted to secure their succession. Joachim's grandson, Joachim Frederick, persuaded the Polish king to give him regency over the mentally unstable Albert in 1603. He also arranged a marriage between his son John (Johann) Sigismund and Albert's daughter, Anna of Prussia, in 1594, disregarding candid warnings from her mother that the duchess wasn't the easiest on the eyes.

As if that wasn't enough, Joachim Frederick went on to marry Anna's younger sister, becoming his son's brother-in-law. Such actions only showcase how contrived and convoluted political marriages were between the nobles of that era. An additional layer of marital and succession complexity came from Anna's female lineage. Her mother was part of the Jülich-Cleves family, which had its own inheritance law that allowed female members to receive titles if there were no other heirs. Thus, because Anna's uncle, who was mentally ill like her father, had no direct heirs, she was next in line to inherit the Jülich-Cleves lands located near the German-Dutch border, around the Rhine River. Of course, Anna's inheritance was far from sure, both for Prussia and for the Jülich-Cleves territories.

First of all, Anna and John weren't the only claimants, and even more troublesome was the fact that neither of the territories adjoined with Brandenburg. Finally, acquiring and holding them required the prince-elector to have the support of his Brandenburgian elites, whose interests were local and had no interest in far-away lands. Trying to compensate for that, in 1605, Joachim Frederick allied himself with the prince-elector of Palatinate, an important noble in the Rhine region. Joachim betrothed his grandson, Georg Wilhelm, to his daughter, which allowed him to become connected with the Dutch, who was a long-time enemy of the Habsburgs, fighting against them since 1560. Furthermore, Palatinate was the center of Calvinism, a more radical form of Protestantism. For the first time, the Hohenzollerns swayed from neutrality and loyalty to the emperor, aligning themselves with the Habsburgs' enemies.

Brandenburg's position soon worsened; in 1608, Joachim Frederick passed away, leaving John to battle for the inheritance of the Jülich-Cleves territories the following year. The religious turbulence of the period led to a clash between the Catholic League and the Protestant Union about the issue, two religion-based alliances of Germanic states. The conflict quickly escalated as the Habsburgs, Dutch, French, and English got involved. In the ensuing chaos, the margrave of Brandenburg was just slightly more than an observer, as his power and wealth were far from competitive with the other major actors. However, John Sigismund himself began further complicating his position in those turbulent times. In 1613, he announced his conversion to Calvinism, a religion that wasn't recognized by the Peace of Augsburg of 1555, leaving him exposed even more. Then, making matters worse, the Protestant Union withdrew its support for his claims in 1617, prompting him to leave the union. In a whirlwind of religious and political struggles, Brandenburg stood alone.

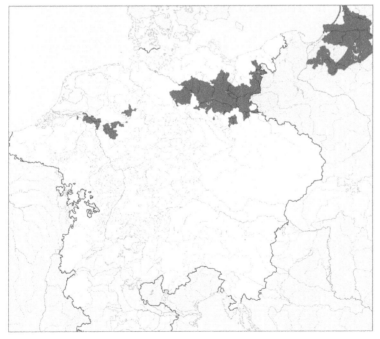

A map showing Brandenburg-Prussia within the Holy Roman Empire in 1618. Source: https://commons.wikimedia.org

As if that wasn't enough trouble for the Hohenzollerns, John's health was quickly declining from his abuse of alcohol and very possibly the stresses caused by the events. He became erratic, obese, and lethargic. Then, in 1616, he suffered a stroke, leaving his speech impaired. It seemed uncertain if he would live long enough to inherit Prussia. Yet, with some luck for his heirs, Duke Albert Frederick died in 1618, activating another claim for John. However, John Sigismund quickly passed it to his son, Georg Wilhelm, as he died in 1619. Prussia and Brandenburg then entered into a personal union under Georg's rule, creating the first outlines of a state that would become known as Prussia, one of Europe's leading powers in later centuries. Nonetheless, at that moment, the future of Brandenburg-Prussia and the Hohenzollerns seemed far from certain, as the Holy Roman Empire and large chunks of Europe got involved in the Thirty Years' War (1618–1648).

Chapter 2 – Rising from the Ashes

Just as the Brandenburg-Prussian union was coming to fruition after almost a century of careful planning by several generations of the Hohenzollern dynasty, a storm appeared above the Holy Roman Empire. With the rising competition between the Catholics and the Protestants, the empire slowly descended into conflict, which grew from a religious confrontation into a power struggle between the major European powers. Unfortunately for the Hohenzollerns, Brandenburg was caught up in the middle of it.

The war began in 1618, just as Albert Frederick passed away, leaving Brandenburg with two unsolved claims. Its inception was when Protestant Bohemia (the modern-day Czech Republic) rose up against the Catholic Habsburg rule, trying to install a Calvinist king on the throne. The war quickly spread across the Holy Roman Empire, as local princes, dukes, and counts swore fealty to either side.

Amidst the chaos, Prince-elector Georg Wilhelm tried to return the Hohenzollerns to neutrality. He avoided fully committing himself to any alliance or side, often relying solely on moral support or empty promises. However, such neutrality could only be upheld with military backing, something none of the Hohenzollern estates provided. In the anarchic and violent clashes of the Thirty Years' War, an unspoken rule was "either you're with us or against us." Thus, Georg Wilhelm's attempts at impartiality left him more or less against everyone.

First, in 1623, a part of the Jülich-Cleves territories that were under Georg's control was invaded by the Protestant League, despite his supposed neutrality. Then, three years later, as he was trying to raise some money to gather at least some troops, parts of Brandenburg were invaded by the Danes, who entered the war on the Protestant side. Despite sharing the same religious beliefs, Brandenburg suffered heavy looting. Soon afterward, imperial troops entered Brandenburg, forcing the margrave to swear fealty to the emperor. Yet, the looting continued, just at the hand of a different army. Simultaneously, the Duchy of Prussia was invaded by Sweden, which used it as a base against Poland. Making matters even more complicated, Georg's sister was married to King Gustavus Adolphus of Sweden. Their connection became even more troubling for the prince-elector around 1630 when Sweden became involved with the Holy Roman Empire's war.

Georg Wilhelm once again tried to return to neutrality, yet the Swedish army marched toward Berlin. Gustavus Adolphus forced Georg into an alliance by giving him an ultimatum. Besides that, the imperial massacre of the Protestant city of Magdeburg in 1631 also helped the margrave to decide. In the summer of that year, Brandenburg-Prussia became a Swedish ally, giving Sweden monetary tribute and the right to its lands for military purposes. In return, the prince-elector was promised parts of Pomerania, a region on the Baltic coast between the Recknitz and Vistula Rivers.

However, the initial Swedish supremacy was cut down by Gustavus's death in 1632, and by 1635, the Habsburgs were once again a winning party. This led Georg Wilhelm to switch sides once again. In return, the emperor promised to honor the claim on

Pomerania. Nevertheless, the Swedes were still a force to be reckoned with, and in 1636, they returned to Brandenburg as the enemy, which was ravaged by both the Swedish and imperial armies. Unable to fend for himself, Georg Wilhelm fled to the Duchy of Prussia, where he hid until his death in 1640.

Later generations of the Hohenzollern rulers deemed Georg Wilhelm to be a bad and indecisive ruler, ascertaining that if he had been succeeded by another ruler like him, both the dynasty and Brandenburg would have been lost to obscurity. Parts of these claims are based on the fact that Brandenburg-Prussia was at its lowest point under Georg's reign. It suffered unimaginable destruction and death. Its population was ravaged, in some regions losing more than 50 percent of its populace. In extreme cases, some smaller towns were completely abandoned. People were starving and dying, suffering atrocities from numerous conquerors and plagued by illnesses and disease. Brandenburg's modest economy was also on the brink, with certain areas losing up to 50 to 60 percent of their farms to destruction and desertion. However, considering the tough position in which Georg Wilhelm was put in, it is questionable how much better a more capable leader could have actually done.

Georg Wilhelm (top) and his son Frederick William, the Great Elector (bottom). Source: https://commons.wikimedia.org

Brandenburg was surrounded by hostile states that were seeking solely to exploit it, and Brandenburg had little capability to fend for itself. This was partially caused by Georg's timid and indecisive nature, which had been caused by a wound from a hunting accident in his youth. However, his choices were, in reality, always between two evils, making his hesitations more than reasonable. Furthermore, he faced substantial opposition from within. His own aristocratic subjects often refused to aid him in money, troops, and other resources, showing little care for Brandenburg's survival. Part of their disagreement came from the fact they were mostly Lutheran while the elector was a Calvinist. Initial disagreements became less important as the war and occupation crushed what little administration existed before it. The margrave's position was only more impaired by the actions and stances of the women of his court, whose religious beliefs narrowed his diplomatic scope. His wife was a passionate Calvinist, while his mother was a devoted Lutheran, both of whom used their personal and familial connections to steer the Hohenzollerns against the Catholic Habsburgs. Thus, when assessing Georg Wilhelm's rule, all of these aggravating circumstances only emphasized his faults. Had he ruled in more peaceful times, he may have been a decent enough ruler. Nonetheless, fate pushed him into a chaos that few could navigate successfully.

Luckily for the Hohenzollerns, his son and heir proved to be a more than capable successor. Frederick William (Friedrich Wilhelm) ascended to the throne in 1640 at the age of twenty, having been shielded from all the death and destruction for most of his childhood. His earliest days were spent in a secure fortress, focused on learning. Then, at the age of fourteen, he was sent to some relatives in the Dutch Republic, which was going through its golden age of naval and economic supremacy. Frederick William's time there seemed to have influenced him the most, as he strived to emulate its success. He wanted to impose the rule of law and impose the state as the guarantee of order, along with a robust financial system that could support the government. Throughout his reign, the prince-elector continuously tried to base Brandenburg's economy on maritime trade as the Dutch did for themselves. Finally, while in the Dutch Republic, he had seen that the republic had well-trained and well-organized troops, which he realized was needed if there was to be peace and stability for Brandenburg-Prussia.

However, all these ideas would have fallen flat if it was not for two important distinctions between Frederick William and his predecessors. One was a sharp mind, trained by years of schooling and learning. The other, probably the most important, was his diligence. He saw his role as the prince-elector not merely as a prestigious title aligned with a bundle of rights and revenues and packed in a bale of ceremonies and formalities. Instead, Frederick William thought of it as his job, a vocation that required all his time and effort. Thus, he worked hard on fulfilling his duties and responsibilities. Arguably, his success stemmed from this more than any other quality he may have had. Nevertheless, his early years on the throne proved the most difficult, especially as the young Frederick William had no actual experience in governing and had to contend with the Thirty Years' War on top of that.

The young prince-elector remained "confined" to his Prussian estate for the first three years of the rule, returning to Brandenburg for the first time in years in 1643. There, he found destruction and misery, as various stragglers and bandits continued to plague the lands even after the Swedish retreated around 1642. In those early years of his reign, Frederick focused on enlarging his army, managing to expand it from a measly three thousand men in 1642 to about eight thousand around 1645. Though still small compared to other forces, it was a considerable increase for Brandenburg-Prussia. A strong army was also vital if the state was to survive, as the prince-elector and his advisors feared that the Polish would seize Prussia as soon as possible. In addition, the Swedes were still present in

Pomerania, while relations with the Habsburgs were still rocky. Even the westernmost Cleves was under threat from the Dutch and French. Luckily for the Hohenzollerns, by the 1640s, most of Europe was tired of what seemed to be an unending war. After years of preparations and then negotiations, the Peace of Westphalia was signed in 1648, ending the prolonged conflict.

The main negotiators for the peace were the Habsburgs, both the Austrian and Spanish branches; France, which entered the war at a later stage; Sweden; Denmark; and the Dutch Republic, along with dozens of smaller state representatives, like the one hailing from Berlin. Those delegations had little sway over matters, but thankfully for Frederick William, France decided to back his claims in an attempt to curb Habsburg power. As such, delegates from Paris agreed with their Swedish allies that the prince-elector would gain eastern parts of Pomerania, honoring, in part, previous agreements with Frederick's father. Then, the two allies pressed the Holy Roman emperor to grant the margrave the former bishoprics of Magdeburg, Halberstadt, Kammin, and Minden as compensation for losing western Pomerania to Sweden. The treaty also confirmed the Hohenzollern rule over the Cleves part of the Jülich-Cleves territories. These acquisitions proved to be vital for the development of Brandenburg-Prussia, as they closed the gap between the central provinces while also making Brandenburg-Prussia the second-largest state of the Holy Roman Empire after the Habsburg estate.

After the war ended, the prince-elector continued his work on establishing a more substantial standing army. He modernized its armaments by introducing lighter and faster firing flintlocks and standardized artillery calibers while also prompting his paid troops to go through constant training and exercise. In establishing a cadet school, Frederick created a constant and stable officer cadre, as well as a standardized professional army formation. All of these military reforms had come from the successful practices of the French,

Dutch, Swedes, and even the imperial army. The crowning achievement was the 1655 establishment of the general war commissioner (*General-kriegkommissar*), which was modeled on recent French reforms. The new office was tasked with overseeing the administrative needs of the army. The office of a war commissioner was supposed to be temporary, and its command wasn't spread equally across the Hohenzollern estates. Nevertheless, over the decades, it expanded both in its territorial reach as well as in prerogatives, slowly decreasing the importance of local nobles in military matters. Despite that, the war commissioner remained a relatively small institution, yet it was, in a way, the inception of the famous Prussian General Staff of later times.

The war commissioner's first "temporary" task was to handle the army's needs in the so-called Second Northern War (1655–1660) between Sweden and Poland, as well as their various allies. The conflict was, in essence, Gustavus's heir's attempt to emulate his predecessor by taking more lands from Poland, among them the Duchy of Prussia, which was still legally a Polish fief. In early 1656, Frederick William tried to negotiate his way out of another threat by allying with the Swedes while gaining full sovereignty of the duchy in return. By that time, the military reforms had increased the Brandenburg-Prussian Army to about twenty-five thousand well-trained soldiers. They, together with the prince-elector himself, proved their worth in the Battle of Warsaw in the summer of that year. The joint Swedish-Prussian army, about eighteen thousand strong, managed to defeat the Polish, who had a force over twice as large. The participation of Frederick's soldiers finally convinced the Swedish to give in to his demands for Prussia's sovereignty. However, the war quickly turned, as the Polish got aid from the Habsburgs and Denmark. Now, the prince-elector sought to gain the same concession from the other side.

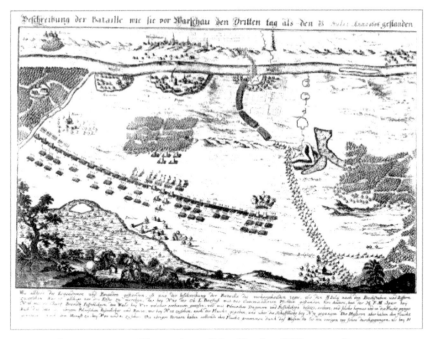

Contemporary illustration of the Battle of Warsaw. Source:
https://commons.wikimedia.org

His military success made him a worthy ally, especially since the Polish king sought to break apart the Swedish-Brandenburg alliance in fear of their connection, as well as the growing threat from Russia. Another important occurrence was the death of the Habsburg emperor in 1657, which allowed the prince-elector to trade his vote for support on the matter. Eventually, joint pressure forced the Polish king to accept Frederick's terms; thus, in September 1657, the Duchy of Prussia became an independent land, with its full sovereignty in Frederick William's hands. In the following two years, he and his army proved their worth some more, playing an important role in ousting the Swedes from the Baltic coast. By 1660, the sides began their negotiations, where the prince-elector hoped to secure the rest of Pomerania for himself. However, his claims were shut down by the French, who claimed that such an event would be in breach of the Peace of Westphalia. France wanted Sweden to maintain its presence in the north, as it would act as a constant threat to France's Habsburg rivals. This taught Frederick William that military strength could only carry him to a certain degree; after all, in the grander European picture, Brandenburg-Prussia was seen as a minor actor.

After such a diplomatic failure, the prince-elector realized that alliances were as important as his armies. Thus, through the 1660s and early 1670s, he utilized Brandenburg-Prussia's position as an important regional partner, switching his allegiances between France and Austria and milking them both for additional monetary subsidies needed for maintaining and further increasing his armies. Then, in 1672, the Franco-Dutch War erupted. With Frederick William's western provinces threatened, he aligned himself with the Habsburg emperor, who instinctively sought to curb French expansion. Nevertheless, the prince-elector maintained contact with Paris, keeping his option open. However, his position was firmly set in December 1674 when the traditional French ally of Sweden invaded Brandenburg, starting the so-called Scanian War. Frederick William rushed back from campaigning in the west, bringing only a fraction of his troops with him. The memory of the Thirty Years' War was still fresh, and he intended to prevent a repeat of that occupation scenario.

The prince-elector, along with roughly six thousand soldiers, arrived home by early summer. Once there, he quickly pounced at the invaders, whose main army numbered roughly eleven thousand men. After some smaller clashes, Frederick William managed to force the Swedes into a major confrontation in the Battle of Fehrbellin. Despite the Swedes' numerical advantage, he managed to outmaneuver them so that they were unable to commit all of their forces to the battle. The Brandenburgians managed to rout the enemy in a single afternoon. The battle itself had minor casualties, roughly five hundred on both sides. However, the Swedes found themselves beset by vengeful peasants and a pursuing army, so they lost many more during the retreat in the following days. Soon,

Brandenburg was free of invaders, allowing its prestige grew. The battle was later characterized as the final breaking point of the mythical "invincible" Swedish army, while the later Hohenzollerns tended to overplay its importance. They used it to mark the mythical inception of the supposedly unbeatable Prussian military. Even Frederick William realized the propaganda value of such a victory. Utilizing the fact that he personally led the army, he began referring to himself as the "Great Elector." From then on, this battle was seen and represented as the point of Prussian rebirth, as it emerged as an important European power.

However, the reality was far from such grandeur. Over the next couple of years, the Great Elector managed to take control of the entire Swedish Pomerania once again by winning more battles. Yet, when the Franco-Dutch War ended in 1678, the major powers were bent on ending the Scanian War as well. In 1679, France more or less dictated that all territory lost by Sweden during the war should be returned. The Habsburgs agreed, as they, too, were more in favor of having a weak Sweden than a strong Brandenburg. Frederick William's hands were tied, as, even with his roughly 38,000 soldiers, he wasn't a match to the French Army, which had roughly 250,000 men. Despite all his achievements, both the Great Elector and Brandenburg-Prussia were still a second-rate power. Thus, after the war ended, Frederick was forced to return to his "pendulum alliance policy," quickly changing allegiances and searching to extort as much money as he could.

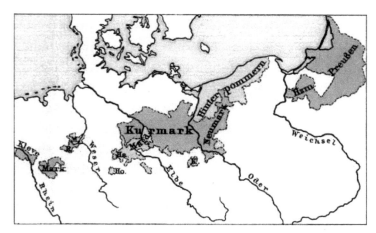

A map depicting Brandenburg-Prussian territory in 1640 (red) and its territorial expansion by 1688 (green). Source: https://commons.wikimedia.org

Looking solely from that viewpoint, it seemed like not much had changed from his father's reign. However, the Great Elector's alliance policy was of his own choice. While Georg Wilhelm was forced by others to switch allegiances, Frederick William did that to benefit himself. Furthermore, under his reign, the economy managed to not only recover but expand to new heights. He used his connection with the Dutch (he was married to a member of the Orange family) to attract artisans, builders, farmers, and traders from the Lowlands, who brought modern technologies and methods with them. Then, in 1685, Frederick opened up his borders for about twenty thousand Huguenots who had fled France in fear of persecution, which also helped with the economic development of the Hohenzollern lands. Furthermore, the Great Elector tried to get Brandenburg involved in the Atlantic "triangular trade" by establishing both the Brandenburg-Prussian navy and the Brandenburg African Company (later renamed the Brandenburg African American Company), which were both modeled after the Dutch, in the 1680s. Despite the failure of maritime and colonial ambitions, during his long reign, Frederick William managed to create an economic basis for the future Prussian state.

Apart from economic development, Frederick also worked on establishing a working state administration. First, he created the position of the Officer of Domains (*Amtskammer*), who was tasked with administering his personal estates. Then, he founded tax commissioners, which, in turn, led to the creation of local administrations headed by a governor who was elected by the regional nobility. Furthermore, Frederick William worked on curbing the power and rights of the nobility by isolating them and pitting them against each other in blind pursuit of their local needs, allowing his power as the head of state to grow. He also incorporated gifted and capable lowborn individuals into the government, as well as in the army, creating the seed for the future Prussian ideal of merit. Nevertheless, in the end, Frederick William's most important and influential achievement was gaining full sovereignty of the Duchy of Prussia, which was to become the cornerstone of the entire Brandenburg-Prussia.

In May of 1688, Frederick William passed away after forty-eight years on the throne, leaving the fate of Brandenburg-Prussia in the hands of his son, now Prince-elector Frederick III. Similar to the previous succession, the new ruler differed greatly from his predecessor. He lacked most of the qualities his father had, something the Great Elector never hid from his son (Frederick William called his son a disappointment). In fact, Frederick William favored his older brother, Charles (Karl) Emil, who showed great talent, charisma, and military aptitude. However, Charles died during the Franco-Dutch War, leaving Frederick next in line for the throne. Unlike his brother, Frederick was sensitive, temperamental, and lacked fighting prowess, mostly due to a childhood injury. Frederick III, who was slightly paranoid, even feared the rest of his family was out to get him in the last years of his father's life, hiding with his in-laws in Hanover. Thanks to this familial disharmony and his clashes with his predecessor, Frederick wasn't properly introduced to state affairs or the hardships of ruling.

As if that wasn't enough, the Great Elector left a testament that ordered the partition of the Hohenzollern lands, as he wished to leave some inheritance for his children from his second marriage. Thus, Frederick's first years on the throne were focused on negating this, calling upon the dynasty succession laws of previous centuries. Only by the early 1690s did he manage to secure his primacy. Nevertheless, the new prince-elector, who was in his thirties, knew exactly what he wanted. He aimed at receiving a kingly title, building upon his father's legacy. His plans hinged upon the fact that Prussia was legally outside of the Holy Roman Empire, as imperial law generally forbade the title of king (the Kingdom of Bohemia was an exception due to its complicated history and ties with the Habsburg dynasty). In the second half of the 1690s, Frederick began various negotiations, trying to find a diplomatic solution to fulfill his goal. Finally, a ripe opportunity arose in late 1700 when the Spanish Habsburg king died without an heir, sparking the War of the Spanish Succession (1701–1714).

A Brandenburgian coin of Frederick I from 1691. Source: https://commons.wikimedia.org

While Holy Roman Emperor Leopold I of House Habsburg prepared for the war, Frederick asked him for the royal crown of Prussia in return for sending eight thousand soldiers for the conflict. He claimed that since Prussia was never a part of the empire, there was no legal obstacle for him to be crowned. A compromise was made when Leopold agreed that Frederick could become the "king

mend it. Simultaneously, the plague increased his resolve to further strengthen the Brandenburg-Prussian Army while also increasing its independence from foreign subsidies. This feeling came from the fact that the disease was brought by passing Russian and Swedish troops during the Great Northern War (1700–1721), which disregarded Prussian neutrality while its troops were tied up in the War of the Spanish Succession. Thus, the great crisis of his father's reign was the catalyst for Frederick William's two most important legacies: reforms of the military and state administration.

A painting of Frederick William I. Source: https://commons.wikimedia.org

Nevertheless, he respected his father's wishes, giving him a grand funeral. Yet, within days afterward, Frederick William began his work on overhauling the entire Hohenzollern state. First, he cleared up all the unnecessary expenditures, starting with the court. Roughly two-thirds of the courtiers were fired, while the rest received pay cuts. He then sold off all unnecessary belongings, like jewelry, lavish coaches, gold plates, fine wines, and various expensive and exotic animals. The court became barer and rougher, with a notably increased atmosphere of militarism and masculinity. What little social life there was in Frederick William's court revolved around the so-called Tobacco Ministry, a group of roughly ten men, mostly councilors and high-ranking officers, who were sometimes joined by visiting envoys or adventurers. Those guests spent evenings with the king, drinking strong liquors and smoking pipes while discussing topics openly and without concern for the usual court hierarchy. In such an atmosphere, there was no room for female influences like there had been in the Hohenzollern courts for centuries, nor for any kind of formalities that had been so cherished by Frederick I.

Similar cuts and reorientations happened outside the court as well. Artists of various sorts began leaving Berlin, leaving some of their work unfinished. Frederick William also cut the funding of his father's academies. He had little tolerance for expenditures in culture and science, as it showed no immediate practical effect; instead, he thought the money should be spent on the military. Such frugality and martial orientation shined through while he was still a prince. Trying to make the Prussian military more practical, in 1707, young Frederick William proposed more uniformity in the arms and gear the army used. This went from gun caliber and bayonets to cartridge pouches. This would allow for easier supplying and interunit sharing of equipment. He also introduced more rigorous parade drills to his own unit, increasing its maneuverability and fire focus. After his ascension, such practices spread to the rest of the Brandenburg-Prussian Army. However, these advances pale in comparison with the achievements Frederick William made in the realm of enlarging his army.

Initially, the king tried to swell his military by forced recruitment done by his officers. However, the use of fear and violence that usually followed such practices quickly exhibited more harm than improvement. By 1714, Frederick William had decided to bolster his recruitment by using logic and order, combined with one's duty toward the state. First, he proclaimed that all able-bodied men had a duty to serve in the army, then he organized regiments by districts or cantons. Units were filled first with volunteers, then supplemented by enlisted men. However, once in the army, men weren't fully removed from their previous lives. They would pass initial training then move into the reserves, where they stayed until retirement. Soldiers would maintain their efficiency by yearly training, which lasted for about two to three months a year, but they would otherwise be free. Thus, military service wouldn't provide much of an economic burden on the state, as reservists could return to their jobs and occupations. With such a policy, Frederick William doubled the size of the Brandenburg-Prussian Army, swelling it to about eighty thousand strong.

Such numbers, combined with a large pool of reservists, meant that his military was the fourth largest in size in Europe. This was rather remarkable considering that Brandenburg-Prussia was tenth in territory and fourteenth in population. With this, his army became self-sufficient in terms of recruitment, while most others still relied upon mercenaries and foreign conscripts. That fact didn't go unnoticed, prompting Frederick William to ban his nobles from entering into foreign service without his specific approval. Prussians were not going to be European mercenaries anymore. Furthermore, he created an institution of a noble cadet school, requiring, more or less, each aristocratic family to give at least one of their members as officers for the army. However, despite occasional objections, most noble families accepted this rather than opposed it. Not only did such a practice give an opportunity for additional income, which was especially important to impoverished aristocrats, it also provided an opportunity to be close to the throne. Thus, this action simultaneously pacified the nobility and directed them to work for the state instead of against it.

Finally, both the aristocratic officer corps and the cantonal system created a heightened sense of honor and duty among the troops. For the nobles, it provided them with an honorable calling, comparable with the aristocratic ideals of the Middle Ages. For the commoners, it created a sense of comradery, as they served with people they knew from their villages and towns. Furthermore, all reservists were required to wear their uniforms in churches and at other important social gatherings, increasing their sense of pride and unity whilst constantly parading symbols of the state. Thus, such prominent militantism increased the nation's sense of loyalty and patriotism. In the end, Frederick William's military reforms were based on the ideas of universal conscription—an ideal that everyone should serve the state. However, that ideal was never fully achieved, as only about one-seventh of eligible men were ever enlisted. Despite that, it set a strong foundation for later military expansion and further reforms for which the Prussian state became famous.

Surprisingly, regardless of the impressive military reforms, Brandenburg-Prussia was only involved in war once during Frederick William's reign. In 1715, he entered the Great Northern War as a Russian ally, attacking Sweden. While the peace with the Swedes was signed in 1720, the actual campaign was more or less done by 1716. During that short period of time, the Hohenzollern king gained the southern part of Swedish Pomerania, most notably the port city of Stettin (modern-day Szczecin). The war itself continued roughly another year before Russia and Sweden signed a peace treaty. With that, Sweden was ousted from Germany and the Baltic coast, which helped to add Prussia's importance as a local ally.

The only other territorial change during Frederick William's reign was the sale of Brandenburg-Prussian colonies in West Africa to the Dutch. For him, colonial adventures were nothing but the fanciful thinking of his predecessors. Thus, despite being nicknamed the "Soldier King" for his reforms, Frederick William I was rather non-belligerent. Such an attitude could be explained by his frugality, as waging war was costly and would most certainly put a dent into his painstakingly built army.

While thriftiness prevented Frederick William from attaining military glory, it motivated him to pursue probably his most impactful legacy: administrative and fiscal reforms. His grandfather, Frederick William, the Great Elector, began transforming the state bureaucracy, yet this momentum was lost during King Frederick I's reign, as he had little interest in such matters. However, King Frederick William I immediately began working on administrative reforms. In a matter of weeks upon his ascension to the throne, he created the General Directory of War and Finance (*Generalfinanzdirektorium*). This was done by merging the Chief Domains Directory, which managed the crown lands, and the Central Revenue Office to form a body that would oversee income from the royal domains. The financial administration was supplemented with the General Commissariat (*Generalkommissariat*), which was tasked with gathering taxes from towns outside of the crown's territories. However, since their jurisdictions and responsibilities often overlapped, the two offices often confronted each other. To solve this problem, in 1723, Frederick William simply merged the two into a "super-ministry" nicknamed the General Directory (*Generaldirektorium*). It was a shortened form of the General Directory of War and Finance.

Autographed instruction of Frederick William I of Prussia for the
Generaldirektorium. *Source: https://commons.wikimedia.org*

Despite the unwieldy name, the office was quite thought-out. On top of the bureaucratic chain stood the ministerial college, while below them were several departments filled with numerous councilors. The most important decisions were made in a joint council with all the ministers and related department representatives. A single chair was always left vacant for the king, but he rarely attended those meetings. Nevertheless, collegial decision-making, in theory, minimized the possibility of one misusing their position while also balancing out various local and personal political interests and needs. Despite sounding like a relatively modern bureaucratic apparatus, the General Directory still lacked some improvements. For example, department jurisdictions weren't streamlined. Thus, one department oversaw the territory of Kumark and Magdeburg while also being in charge of provisioning and quartering the troops. Furthermore, with these blurred lines between departments, there were plenty of internal clashes within the directory. Nevertheless, it marked the modernization of the state apparatus.

Such a transformation was important both for increased government revenue and efficiency, as well as for battling the aristocracy's influence. Frederick William purposefully looked at competent commoners to fill various roles in the General Directory, from local positions and offices all the way up to the higher ranks. Thus, he prevented the government from having a sense of solidarity with the nobles. Of course, there were always capable aristocrats willing to assist him in those ventures, whether it was for personal designs or the need for a salary. However, the king in Prussia didn't merely stop there. He found other ways to curb the nobility's power. One was reforming the land taxes. Until his reign, there was a flat rate that was paid per *Hufe* of land owned. A *Hufe* was a measure of land, similar to the medieval English hide, roughly thirty modern acres. Such taxation ignored the yield variations of farmable lands, and the tax-collecting was also still mostly in the hands of the nobles, who often turned a blind eye to each other.

To rectify this, Frederick William ordered a comprehensive landholding survey. This important task exposed some 35,000 previously untaxed *Hufen*, roughly 2,300 square miles (6,000 square kilometers). Then, a local administration officer went on to create a wide classification list of all the holdings according to their soil quality, allowing for fairer taxation. Finally, the taxation was slowly transferred from the hands of the nobles to the central government. Such reforms not only increased the state's income but also helped the growth of agriculture, as pressure was relieved from the poorest smallholders to the major landowners, who were usually aristocrats. The changes also represented the change in ruling and economic theory. Like many other German economists of the time, Frederick William felt that overtaxation reduced productivity. At the same time, the king felt that one of his duties as a sovereign was to protect his subjects, so he began focusing more on the peasants.

Finally, Frederick William dealt another major blow to the leftovers of the feudal era by once again targeting the nobility's power. While the land was being surveyed, he began the process known as the "allodification of the fiefs." In essence, it was the process of de-feudalization, as the royal bureaucracy planned to clear any residual feudal ties between the crown and the landowners. By legally owning the lands, all historical claims would be lifted, allowing for greater freedoms and incentives for agricultural improvements. However, in return, the owners had to pay taxes. This, once again, targeted mostly the aristocracy, who held various contracts and exemptions given for various reasons in previous centuries. Frederick William made that kind of disregard toward tradition clear from the moment he ascended the throne, as he refused to sign the usual concessions to the provincial aristocracy. In his eyes, such leeway given to the nobles eroded the absoluteness of the monarchical reign, which was, in the end, his ultimate goal.

Apart from administrative and martial reforms, Frederick William also worked on bolstering the economy. Apart from the already mentioned agricultural incentives through taxes and allodial reforms, he followed the basic principles of mercantilism, though in a somewhat different form than the original French economic policy. The king sought to protect local farmers by imposing high import taxes on wheat and cracking down on smuggling. Additionally, he banned the export of wool in an attempt to bolster the local textile industry, which was, at the time, the British Industrial Revolution's main motor. In essence, he wanted to lower the imports and make the Prussian economy more reliable and self-reliant. The main difference from more conventional mercantilists was that Frederick William was focused more on agriculture than manufacturing, and he also ignored the advantages of trade. The complete disregard of foreign trade can be seen in his handling of the African colonies. In internal affairs, he was somewhat interested. During Frederick William's rule, the construction of a system of canals between the Oder and Elbe Rivers was sped up, and he also worked on decreasing internal trade tolls. However, the market unification of all the Brandenburg-Prussian territories was never achieved.

Another important economic and social policy used by Frederick William was population resettlement and, even more important, welcoming religious refugees. Like any reasonable ruler, he realized empty lands and workshops meant a loss of revenue for the state. Thus, he sought to repopulate the demographically devastated eastern Prussia. That practice had begun while his father was still alive, but the new king made it a much more important issue. Thus, the crown provided help for internal migration. Later on, in 1732, he allowed Protestant refugees from Salzburg, roughly twenty thousand of them, to settle. In roughly the same period, Prussia accepted some Bohemian refugees, settling them near Berlin. Like in previous times, these people brought their expertise and skills, creating a small economic boost to the lands they settled. Such policies were not new for Brandenburg-Prussia, but they show the Hohenzollerns' religious tolerance while also filling the losses caused by the plague.

No. XCVII. Verordnung, daß die Eltern ihre Kinder zur Schule, und die Prediger die Catechisationes, halten sollen; vom 28. Sept. 1717.

Von Gottes Gnaden Fridrich Wilhelm, König in Preussen, Marggraff zu Brandenburg, des Heil. Römischen Reichs Ertz-Cämmerer und Chur-Fürst. ꝛc.

Unsern ꝛc. Wir vernehmen mißfällig und wird verschiedentlich von denen Inspectoren und Predigern bey Uns geklaget, daß die Eltern, absonderlich auf dem Lande, in Schickung ihrer Kinder zur Schule sich sehr säumig erzeigen, und dadurch die arme Jugend in grosse Unwissenheit, so wohl was das lesen, schreiben und rechnen betrifft, als auch in denen zu ihrem Heyl und Seeligkeit dienenden höchstnötigen Stücken auffwachsen lassen. Weßhalb Wir umb diesem höchst verderblichen Uebel auff ein mahl abzuhelffen in Gnaden resolviret, dieses Unser General Edict ergehen zu lassen, und darinn allergnädigst und ernstlich zu verordnen,

daß hinkünfftig an denen Orten wo Schulen seyn, die Eltern bey nachdrücklicher Straffe gehalten seyn sollen Ihre Kinder gegen Zwey Dreyer Wochentliches Schuel Geld von einem jeden Kinde, im Winter täglich und im Sommer wann die Eltern die Kinder bey ihrer Wirthschafft benötiget seyn, zum wenigsten ein oder zweymahl die Woche, damit Sie das jenige, was im Winter erlernet worden, nicht gäntzlich vergessen mögen, in die Schuel zuschicken. Falß aber die Eltern das Vermögen nicht hätten; So wollen Wir daß solche Zwey Dreyer aus jeden Orts Allmosen bezahlet werden sollen. Dann wollen und befehlen Wir auch allergnädigst und ernstlich, daß hinführo die Prediger insonderheit auf dem Lande alle Sonntage Nachmittage die Catechefation mit ihren Gemeinden ohnfehlbar halten sollen; Wornach ihr Euch

Euch gehorsamst zu achten, diesen Unsern allergnädigsten Willen und Befehl gehöriger Orten zu publiciren, darüber Nachdrücklich zu halten, auch fisco auff zugeben habt, ein wachsahmes Auge zu haben und die Contravenienten zur Bestraffung anzuzeigen. Daran geschiehet Unser allergnädigster Wille, und Wir

seynd Euch mit Gnaden gewogen. Geben Berlin den 28. Sept. 1717.

Auff Sr. Königl. Majest. allergnädigsten Special-Befehl.

v. Dohnhoff. Ilgen. v. Blaspiel v. Ploteho.

Ordinance on the introduction of compulsory schooling in Prussia in 1717.
Source: https://commons.wikimedia.org

Overall, when judging Frederick William I's reign, one can see it was clearly guided by logic, frugality, and absolutism. He wanted to control every aspect of life in his lands, and he worked diligently, demanding the same from his subordinates. Yet, he never forgot the needs of his subjects, great or small. Thus, he expanded granaries, allowing for more stable prices of grain and ensuring there was no more famine. However, his education policy probably shined the most light on his statesmanship. As it was said, he wasn't very concerned with higher education and culture. To him, it was a waste of money. At the same time, he deemed basic education a necessity for a more productive and ordered society. Thus, in 1717, he proclaimed compulsory basic education, being among the first such acts in history. He wanted his subjects to be able to read, write, and do basic math, and he wasn't afraid to order their children to attend school. Though today that seems like a normal part of life, at the time, it was a serious intrusion of family privacy and parenthood. This was absolute control in the name of efficiency.

A 19ᵗʰ-century representation of the Long Lads Battalion in an infantry charge. Source: https://commons.wikimedia.org

Nevertheless, even a king like Frederick William I allowed had illogical and wasteful ideas. For Frederick William, it was the royal guard nicknamed the Long Lads (*Lange Kerle*), which was composed of men at least 6 feet, 2 inches (1.88 meters) tall. Even today, such height is above average, but at the time, such height was even rarer. In comparison, the king himself was 5 foot, 3 inches (1.60 m), which was more comparable with the average height. Thus, gathering some three thousand men of such stature required investment and a "manhunt" across Europe, from England to Ukraine. Not only was it expensive to bring them to Prussia, but the king also gave them higher salaries and some other benefits. Worst of all, most of them were unfit for actual military duty due to their gigantism. Thus, they were merely a decoration, fit for parades and impressing foreign dignitaries. Despite that, there were many accounts of Frederick William finding solace and joy in watching them march up and down his courtyard.

In the end, King Frederick William I was later seen as a spiritual father of the Prussian state, establishing its administrative and military backbone and allowing for its later expansion. However, by the late 1730s, the king grew ill. He was plagued by gout, which had been brought on by his drinking and genetic disposition, rendering him almost bound to a wheelchair. Frederick William passed away in May of 1740 at the age of fifty-one, most likely from heart failure. He was buried as he lived, in a simple metal sarcophagus without any decorations on it. Nevertheless, the success and reforms of his reign continued to resonate with greatness, inspiring his successors to follow in his footsteps.

Chapter 4 – Changing Society

By the mid-18th century, Brandenburg-Prussia was a rather transformed nation. Over roughly a century and three generations of Hohenzollern rulers, it had moved away from its medieval roots into modernity. It was a rather intentional and purposefully constructed change. However, this trend occurred across Europe, making Prussia just one of the states going through reforms, albeit with their own local uniqueness.

One of the major differences between Brandenburg-Prussia and most of the other European states was its fluid religious policy. Compared to other nations, it seemed quite relaxed, though not without its questionable moments. Complications began in 1613 when John Sigismund accepted Calvinism, making it the official religion of the Hohenzollern dynasty. At the time, the majority in Brandenburg were Lutheran, although there were some remnants of Catholics as well. Since religion played an important role in the people's lives, the two schools of Protestantism quickly clashed over their interpretations of Christianity. Some of the notable differences lay in the ideas of predestination and God's sovereignty. For Lutherans, anyone could attain salvation, and humans had some control over their lives. On the other hand, Calvinists believed that people were preselected for salvation and that God had absolute dominion over one's life. However, although these religious ideas were important to them, this struggle also had a political motivation. Calvinism quickly became the faith of the central government, while the provincial nobility clung to Lutheranism, connecting the religious dispute with the struggle for power and sovereignty.

This prompted Frederick William, the Great Elector, to issue an edict in 1664, proclaiming religious tolerance and forcing towns to accept citizens regardless of their faith. It was an attempt to reconcile the two major congregations. Though forcibly enacted, the edict eased some tensions. However, it wasn't a universal tolerance. Most notably, the Jewish population continued to suffer great religious pressure, which began in the late 16th century. They were expelled from Brandenburg at the time, but with later territorial acquisitions, some smaller communities in Cleve once again fell under the Hohenzollern rule. Nevertheless, the Great Elector chose not to persecute them, but they weren't allowed to move to the electorate. However, in 1671, he allowed a small group of wealthy Jews fleeing from the Habsburgs to settle there. Catholics also had some limits on their faith, though no great purges were ever made. Yet, despite that, Brandenburg-Prussia was still seen as a relatively tolerant state in the late 17th and early 18th centuries. The only actual pressure made by the Hohenzollern rulers was by settling Calvinist emigrants, which, besides economic benefits, bolstered their numbers in a still predominantly Lutheran state.

Yet, despite the ruling dynasty's effort to reconcile Calvinists and Lutherans, discontent brewed beneath the surface. Then, in the late 17th century, a new branch of Lutheranism appeared in Brandenburg-Prussia. It became known as Pietism, and though it still rested on similar principles as the orthodox Lutherans, they argued that faith was individual, that it comes from within, and that, ultimately, there was no need for theological debate. In practice, this made them much more tolerable to other denominations than the "proper" Lutherans. Sensing an opportunity, Frederick III (later

King Frederick I), who was just an elector at the time, embraced them and even helped the Pietists to establish a university in Halle in 1691. This helped Pietism to establish itself, but it also gave the Hohenzollerns new Lutheran allies. It's worth noting that Halle was the largest city in Magdeburg, a region that was a bastion for orthodox Lutherans and opponents of Calvinism. Within a couple of years, Pietist ideas began to spread, and it did, in fact, slightly dull the Lutherans' edge.

Apart from religious policy, Pietism brought other benefits to the state. From their early days in Halle, they were rather active in various social services, providing shelter and food for the poor, creating herbal medicines, and, most importantly, offering free education for the lowest members of society. The latter created foundations for the education system that would spread across Prussia. It was all part of their concern for their fellow Christians and an attempt to create a better society. Thus, the collaboration between the crown and the Pietists continued in the early 18th century. It picked up even more speed with Frederick William I's ascension to the throne. As a child, he had close contact with them and became rather sympathetic to some of their idealized virtues, such as frugality, self-discipline, modesty, and austerity. Those resonated with his visions for a proper society. During his reign, Pietism came under special focus. The king promoted it almost anywhere he could, from bureaucratic apparatus, across the education system, and even in his precious army. They proved to be a significant part of his personal goal to change Brandenburg-Prussia during his rule.

However, the Pietists never managed to overtake other congregations. Their expansion stopped after Frederick William died in 1740, as they had lost their royal support. Even worse, by then, they had lost most of their prominent leaders. Pietism, as a religious movement, lost its momentum. Nevertheless, its cultural importance cannot be underestimated. Though it had a religious core, Pietism put ethics above dogma. It valued punctuality, order, diligence, and modesty, which would all become Prussian core values. Thanks to their ties with education, both in its spreading and reform, these beliefs were spread across the nation. This was, of course, done in no small degree thanks to Frederick William's design. In the end, it was thanks to Pietism that Brandenburg-Prussia laid the ground for the future hallmarks of Prussian and German society while simultaneously paving the path for progressive ideas that would come with the Enlightenment in the latter half of the 18th century.

These ideas and education in general were instrumental in transforming Prussian urban society. The story of this change begins with the authoritarian reforms of the 17th century. However, it is important to realize that the lands ruled by the Hohenzollerns weren't as urban as in some other European regions. For example, around 1700, Brandenburg-Prussia had only two cities with a population of about ten thousand or more: Berlin and Königsberg (modern-day Kaliningrad). Nevertheless, there were dozens of small towns across the Hohenzollern state with their own specific societal milieu. These were run by local master artisans and merchants and were interconnected to form an urban patrician familial network. Their unique identity was garnished by the privileges and degree of autonomy they inherited from medieval times, as cities in Europe generally laid on the edge of the sovereign's control. Thus, the cities were traditionally centers of civic virtues and political self-rule that contrasted to the monarchical system. As the Hohenzollerns strived toward an absolutist reign, towns were their opposition just as much as the nobles.

return for their military service. Because the crown depended so much on them, they had leverage against their rulers, making them the most influential class in the state. The Junkers' importance was only increased by the fact that across Brandenburg-Prussia, they controlled anywhere between 60 to 40 percent of the lands, depending on the region. This was comparable with England, but it was way above the average of France and Russia, whose percentages were 20 or below. It's worth noting that not all of the aristocratic families had large estates; in fact, most of them were rather small compared to their European peers. Nevertheless, using their influence, they often opposed any reforms that curtailed their power. Luckily for the Hohenzollerns, the Junkers of the 17th century were still fragmented and interested only in local affairs, leaving enough space for the crown to maneuver around.

The change in the nature of the Junkers' families came with the militarization of King Frederick William I. Since the nobles were forced to serve in the army and, more importantly, train in the officer corps, the provincial differences began to dissipate. The families from different regions began to intermarry and create connections, making the Junkers a statewide unified class. Theoretically, this should have made them more powerful; however, military service and the possibility of higher salaries through promotions kept many of the less rich nobles loyal. Furthermore, through the cadet school, they were exposed to loyalty-inducing education. From then on, the officer rank became somewhat synonymous with the Junkers. This was only exacerbated during Frederick II's reign, who opposed the promotion of commoners as much as possible. However, the nobility's power was curtailed in the mid-18th century, as an economic crisis and war endangered them. Many of them lost their lives on the battlefield, while others went into debt. Seeking to preserve them, Frederick II created state-backed credit unions. This made many of the Junker families dependent on the state, reversing the balance of power from the 17ᵗʰ century. Thus, from then on, the Junkers became loyal and obedient servants of the Hohenzollern dynasty.

Since the Junkers were an overtly militant class, their representation was usually rather masculine. Their familial ideal was an extended household led by a paterfamilias who would exert his status as the head of the family for the good of the household. With that, it seems there was little space for women to fulfill any significant role besides knitting, gardening, or minding the kitchens. However, there were a number of written sources depicting aristocratic women inheriting estates and taking full control over them. They weren't passive owners nor the legal holder of transferable rights of ownership that would be carried on to their closest male kin. Contrary to expectations, these ladies exercised total control over the estate, developing and investing in it, as well as gathering income; they even served as local judiciaries. However, historical evidence leaves us uncertain about the commonality of these examples. Yet, since the sources never depict women landlords as bizarre or an anomaly, it hints that it was at least socially accepted even if it was not particularly common.

A 1763 portrait of Frederick II. Source: https://commons.wikimedia.org

Interestingly, that kind of status somewhat extended to the commoners as well. Women could be co-owners of estates, especially if it was part of their dowry, while the entire household was usually co-managed in a way that saw wives controlling and managing the family budget. Furthermore, it wasn't uncommon for some better-off commoners to acquire enterprises for their wives, most notably taverns, giving them semi-independency and increasing their social status. However, this doesn't mean there was anything really near equality as we know it today, but rather that, in some ways, Prussian society was a bit more liberal than others at the time. There were still quite stark differences; for example, in the case of adultery and illegitimate children, it was usually seen as the women's fault. Furthermore, city guilds were usually closed to females, making it almost impossible for them to advance in urban artisanal industries. In the countryside, the division between male and female labor was less pronounced, and both sexes worked on the fields as needed. However, as the 18th century was coming to an end, it seems that Prussian society was slowly transforming to a much more conservative one, stifling these hints of equality.

Another unique development in Prussian society was the position of peasants. In the mid-15th century, the Junkers first restructured their estates so that the best land was under their direct control while simultaneously increasing their level of control over their dependents. Most notably, they imposed forced labor and forbade them from leaving the lands. Thus, while the rest of Europe was abandoning feudalism, in Brandenburg-Prussia, there was something close to a feudal revival, albeit with one major distinction. Peasants weren't true serfs since they didn't legally belong to their masters. Such a level of dominion over their subjects often bordered and crossed into tyranny, leaving peasants in poverty and apathy. However, by the 17th century, these conditions began to change, mostly thanks to the state's intervention. Both the Great Elector and his grandson sought to protect the commoners from unjust treatment by their masters. This was done by intertwining the local laws with statewide regulations. Then, Frederick II took it a step beyond by requiring the territorial courts to employ university-educated judges.

It is also vital to note that even without state protection, not all peasants were repressed and abused. There were many cases where, with proper estate management, many Junker families managed to create incentives for work, such as paid labor, which instilled some sense of entrepreneurship among the peasants. On the other side of the spectrum were estates where peasants grouped together to rebel against their lieges. In several instances, the commoners were strong enough to refuse to pay taxes or do proscribed labor. However, these weren't uprisings against the Junkers' rule but rather demonstrations due to unfair treatment, usually the unlawful increase of duties. What seems to be common for all these rebellions was the commoners' utmost trust that the judicial system would ultimately protect them against the oppression of their masters. Another way of peaceful resistance was neglecting the land, which created an impetus for the landowners to employ paid labor and fairer treatment.

Furthermore, by the mid-18th century, there was a considerable number of free peasants. Most of these were settlers and migrants, as well as their descendants. They were most prominent in eastern Prussia because of the plague in the early 18th century. By the end of the century, more than 20 percent of the peasants there were non-subjugated farmers. Overall, it seems that the Hohenzollerns "used" the commoners to further curtail the power of the Junkers, dismantling remnants of feudalism along the way. Immigrants played an additional role in Brandenburg-Prussia. The Hohenzollerns used them to boost manufacturing and industry. Some of them were industrious and versed in such matters, creating a base for further development. However, the crown did more than just invite manufacturers and experts to their lands. Most notably, the state tried to prevent the export of raw materials, giving local producers resources to work with. Besides that, the government and the ruler sought to give subsidies and aid for starting or developing industries in the towns.

First among them was the textile-related industries, namely wool and silk. Then came the leather industry, followed by various factories related to metal products like scissors, knives, and even munition. All this was further boosted with the formation of the iron ore industry after Frederick II gained more territories. All of these industries were heavily protected by import tariffs but also suffered from governmental guidance. According to some historians and even contemporaries, as much as state investments had helped set up the industries, they began to stifle Prussia's progress by the late 18th century. However, despite their claims and even under such conditions, the Prussian industry wasn't really stagnating, nor was it under the all-encompassing control of the state. Most of the factories were privately held, even those connected with military needs, while production continuously increased despite complaints of governmental interloping. Even more important, state funding allowed for the previously economically devastated Brandenburg-Prussia to create a foundation for its later industrial rebirth, allowing Prussia to catch up with British industrial might that was brought about in the 18th-century Industrial Revolution. Furthermore, it led to the formation of a new economic elite, which included industrials, bankers, subcontractors, and distributors.

Overall, when following the trends in the Brandenburg-Prussian society and state, it seems that the late 17th and early 18th centuries was a period of transforming into a modern nation. Some of the changes were intentional, some unintended, but most were connected with the Hohenzollerns' underlying desire to increase either their economic and military power. Despite that, it should be mentioned that, in the larger picture, similar changes were happening across all of western Europe.

Chapter 5 – Pride and Glory

The transformation of the Prussian state and society in the late 17th and early 18th centuries hinted at a new reservoir of power behind the Hohenzollern dynasty. Through various reforms and improvements, a seed of greatness was sown. The first of its blossoms were to bloom with Frederick William's son, King Frederick II, better known as Frederick the Great.

As with his predecessors, the story of Frederick's reign begins with familial traumas during his formative years. While he was still a child, he exhibited a fondness for reading, arts, and philosophy, and he was much less concerned with military issues and certainly less blunt than his father. This irritated Frederick William, who thought that his son and heir should be as close as possible to his mirror image. Hence, the two began constantly clashing. The father imposed a grueling routine upon his son, forcing him to deal with stately affairs before he even became a teenager. When the treatment showed little effect, Frederick William became increasingly frustrated, and he was prone to engage in public ridicule and violence at the expense of his heir. In return, Frederick became colder and more distant; although he was outwardly supportive of his father, privately, he became more inclined toward his own interests. Then, in the late 1720s, young Frederick became a focal point of political machinations in the court. His mother sought to arrange a marriage with Princess Amelia of Britain, but several ministers opposed it. They were most likely bribed by the Habsburgs to prevent such an alliance.

Frederick II (on the window) watching the execution of his friend Katte.
Source: https://commons.wikimedia.org

Frederick William I quickly opposed the marriage, fearing the break with Vienna, while Frederick decided to support his mother's plot. In the end, though, the king's word was final, and the queen had to back down. For his son, this was a tipping point, not because he really cared for Princess Amelia but because of his resentment for his father's actions and treatment of him. This prompted Frederick to attempt to flee the country with the help of a friend and Prussian officer named Hans Hermann von Katte. However, they were caught and imprisoned in the Küstrin fortress. Frederick was sentenced to imprisonment on charges of treason. He would remain at Küstrin, condemned to go through rigorous training in governance and administration. Yet, the true punishment was the execution of his friend and co-conspirator, which he was forced to watch. It showed the extent of his father's cold-heartedness. Despite that, the two worked on reconciling in the following years. In 1732, Frederick was released and reinstituted on the condition he would marry a bride of his father's choosing.

Frederick accepted, but he warned that he would "reject" his wife. Over the next several years, his relationship with Frederick William improved, most notably because his father eased up on him. Frederick was given a castle near Berlin, where he spent most of his time until his ascension to the throne. There, he continued to enjoy and practice the arts, philosophy, and writing, living a life that almost resembled freedom. He didn't only enjoy the works of others but also dabbled in philosophic works, music, and poetry himself. He also worked on political tracts, most notably his essay, the *Anti-Machiavel*, as well as historical manuscripts, such as the *History of House of Brandenburg*. This solidified his erudite personality. It also gave him the possibility to comprehend his role and position in the development of Prussia and the Hohenzollern dynasty. It also allowed him to develop less desirable personality traits for an 18th-century ruler. Frederick became an atheist, claiming that Christianity was merely metaphysical fiction filled with contradictions and absurdities. He was also rumored to be homosexual or at least more inclined to men than women. Such gossip began even during his lifetime, and it is still a highly debated topic even today.

Partially, this was because he remained cold toward his wife, Elisabeth. After 1740, Frederick and Elisabeth had basically separated, though they never divorced. She was sidelined in a single castle, retaining all her official titles and prerogatives, but she was never accepted as part of her husband's social circle. Making matters worse, they never produced an heir, and it seems that their relationship never got to a sexual level. Another conspicuous act was that even after becoming the king, Frederick abstained from having mistresses. That would be a viable "way out" if the marriage was too important to be dissolved. Adding to the speculations was Frederick's inclination toward male company. On its own, this wouldn't be too damning. Even Frederick William had his Tobacco Ministry. However, Frederick's inner circle was less macho-orientated, filled with gentler types like poets and philosophers. Most notoriously, all of them, including the king, dabbled in erotic poetry and essays, some of which hinted at dubious feelings of attraction. Eyebrow-raising relations with the famous philosopher Voltaire only added to the slander. The two of them had rather feisty relations, filled with mutual appreciation and constant bickering. After a falling out, Voltaire even claimed that Frederick enjoyed the company of his lackeys and cadets, though he never went "all the way."

These claims of homosexuality were vigorously combated by German writers and memoirists, who talked about Frederick's mistresses in his youth, hinting that he was heterosexual at the time. In the end, the reality of Frederick's sexuality remains a mystery. It is entirely possible he was either bisexual or asexual, with the latter possibly being the result of his father's ill-treatment. In that case, his sexuality toward both genders would be only artistic and intellectual.

However, the matter of Frederick's sexuality remains less important, as it pales in comparison to his grand achievements. The first glimpses of Frederick's greatness came in 1740, within a few months of him ascending to the throne. In contrast to the peaceful reign of his father, the "Soldier King," twenty-eight-year-old Frederick II began his rule with a declaration of war against the Habsburgs.

A map of Europe in 1740. Source: https://commons.wikimedia.org

Despite being mocked for his lack of military prowess, King Frederick II realized that the time was ripe to attack Austria. Firstly, the Habsburgs' treasury was running dry after having lost a couple of their previous wars. When Frederick was still the crown prince, he took part in one of them as a leader of a Prussian contingent. It allowed him to witness firsthand how inferior the Austrian army was compared to his father's troops. Moreover, in late 1740, Emperor Charles VI died, leaving only daughters. His principal heir was Maria Theresa, whose right to inherit as a female was questionable, to say the least, as Habsburgs law dictated male primogeniture. Her father tried to secure Maria's inheritance with an edict, but that wasn't enough to restrain numerous Austrian opponents. This added to Frederick's opportunity; not only would other German dynasties try to achieve gains, but he knew that France wouldn't mind if the Habsburgs were taken down a notch. Furthermore, Britain and Russia, which were chief Austrian allies, were preoccupied with their own issues.

Thus, acting quickly, in December 1740, Frederick started the so-called First Silesian War, named after Prussia's primary target. He attacked, acting on flimsy Hohenzollern claims on Silesia that dated back to the 16th and early 17th centuries. However, these were just a pretext for a war of pure aggression. The real reason Silesia was his primary target came from the fact that it was the only Habsburg region bordering Brandenburg-Prussia. Adding to that was the fact that it was lightly defended, as the majority of the Habsburg troops were deployed elsewhere. It was only a bonus that it was also the richest and most valuable Habsburg province, yielding high taxes and a rather developed industry. The final motive was the threat of Saxony trying to conquer Silesia. This would, in turn, threaten Brandenburg, as it would connect Saxony and Poland, which were under the personal union of Frederick Augustus from the Wettin dynasty. If the Wettins took Silesia, they would more or less encircle the Hohenzollerns, making their future questionable, to say the least.

The war began auspiciously. The Prussian troops easily swept the Habsburg defenders, taking control of almost all of Silesia by January 1741. In the spring, the Austrians gathered for a counterattack. They had some minor success, but in the Battle of Mollwitz, their momentum was broken by a Prussian victory. At that moment, other European nations felt the Habsburgs' weakness. An alliance between France, Spain, Bavaria, and Saxony was formed, along with Brandenburg-Prussia. The allies confirmed Frederick's claim and conquest, and their entrance started a much larger conflict known as the War of the Austrian Succession. The campaigns continued throughout late 1741 and early 1742, with the Prussian Army playing an active role in it. However, by the summer, Frederick sensed it was enough for him and Prussia. He had achieved his goal and wasn't keen on totally dismembering Austria to replace it with some other new power. Thus, he negotiated a separate peace through the treaties of Breslau and Berlin. Maria Theresa had little choice but to cede Silesia to the Hohenzollerns.

Despite gaining roughly one million new subjects and around 14,000 square miles (35,000 square kilometers), Frederick continued to monitor the situation in the ongoing European conflict. He was wary of a possible renewed threat from Austria, as he was certain it wasn't going to abandon Silesia that easily. By mid-1744, Frederick realized his position might be threatened. The war had turned. France had suffered severe setbacks, while Austria formed alliances with Britain, Russia, and Saxony. Frederick was aware he had to act quickly. After signing some more treaties with France and other Germanic states, Prussia reentered the arena. This renewed conflict became known as the Second Silesian War. Initially, it seemed it was going to be a repeat of the first campaign, as the Prussians managed to quickly invade Habsburgian Bohemia, taking Prague in the process. However, due to France's weakness at the time, the Austrians managed to redeploy their soldiers back to the east. Faced by the joint Austro-Saxon army, as the latter became an active belligerent, by November 1744, Frederick was forced to retreat. This not only harmed his military reputation but also cost him a substantial chunk of his army, as low supplies and illnesses reduced it by half.

A later painting of the Battle of Hohenfriedberg. Source: https://commons.wikimedia.org

In early 1745, the Austrians refocused on subduing Bavaria before once again targeting Prussia with their Saxon allies. Frederick waited for them with a replenished army in Silesia. The first major encounter happened in June at the Battle of Hohenfriedberg. Both armies were roughly the same size, around sixty thousand, but the Prussians' training and Frederick's command tipped the scale in his favor. The Austro-Saxon army fled, and Frederick went on the pursuit. However, over the next two months, no major battles occurred as he tried to secure another peace that would confirm Prussian control over Silesia. However, Maria Theresa wasn't ready to give up yet, even though she was losing British support due to their own internal issues at the time. Then, in late September, the Austro-Saxon army decided to challenge the pursuers. By then, the Prussian Army had less than twenty-five thousand men, making it seem like perfect prey for the forty thousand Austro-Saxon troops. The latter even tried to make their clash a surprise attack near the village of Soor. Despite all of their disadvantages, the Prussian troops still managed to win the battle. Frederick hoped that this defeat would be enough for the Habsburgs to sue for peace, but their resolve was unscathed.

While the Prussians retreated to Silesia to regroup and resupply, the Austrians and Saxons agreed to take the war to Brandenburg. Their goal was to seize Berlin and end the war altogether. However, Frederick got wind of their plans, and he arranged for a new defensive army in his homeland while silently following the Austro-Saxons with his army. He waited until they arrived at the Brandenburgian border before attacking them in late November. The Battle of Hennersdorf was yet another crushing defeat for the coalition forces. Frederick's other army then marched into Saxony, with both Prussian forces converging on its capital of Dresden. The second Prussian force then found a smaller army of mostly Saxon soldiers on its way. Despite being slightly outnumbered, with thirty-five thousand Austro-Saxons against some thirty-two thousand Prussians, the latter decided to attack. Once again, Prussian leadership and troop quality led to a crushing victory in mid-December 1745 at the Battle of Kesselsdorf. A few days later, the

Prussian troops entered Dresden. There was no other option for the Austro-Saxon alliance than to accept Frederick's terms.

Mediated by the British, the Treaty of Dresden was signed on December 25th, 1745, ending the Second Silesian War. The end result was another confirmation of Prussian gains in Silesia, which had been Frederick's primary goal, and the Saxons also had to pay a hefty indemnity. In return, Prussia acknowledged Maria Theresa's husband as the emperor. The grander conflict of the War of the Austrian Succession lasted for almost another three years, ending in late 1748. That peace treaty once again confirmed that Silesia was now Prussian, despite the fact that it wasn't involved in the war, nor was Frederick even one of the signees. By now, Frederick II was gaining his nickname "the Great," as he shocked the other powers with his decisive victories. Just a few years before, it was unimaginable that the third-rate power of Brandenburg-Prussia would be able to beat one of the leading world powers, the Habsburgs. This caused a ripple effect in the rearranging of alliances, as Prussia had emerged as one of the leading Germanic powers, directly challenging Habsburgian dominance within the Holy Roman Empire.

The most notable change was that Maria Theresa decided to go against the Habsburg traditions and tried to align itself with France rather than Britain. This caused the so-called Diplomatic Revolution, as the main axis of alliances was aligned around long-lasting hostilities between the Habsburgs and the French Bourbons. This change was done partially when Austria realized its interests and geopolitical position were vastly different than Britain. However, it was also partially aimed against Prussia. Regaining Silesia became one of the Habsburgs' primary goals, not only for its economic importance but also for the loss of prestige. While the alliances slowly shifted, the French and British began clashing over their colonial possessions in North America. Britain anticipated a full-out war and concluded a treaty with Russia to attack Prussia in order to halt Frederick as a French ally from taking over Hanoverian lands on the continent. This alarmed the king in Prussia, who immediately tried to negotiate a deal with the British. Thus, by early 1756, Brandenburg-Prussia became a British ally and swore to protect King George II's lands in Hanover.

It was a rash action, mostly caused by Frederick's gross fear of a Russian invasion. He miscalculated his move so much that it played straight into the vengeful hands of the Habsburgs. The French saw it as a betrayal of their continuing alliance, while the Russians were angry about the treatment. Both were ready to ally with Austria against Prussia. A storm was brewing on the horizon, and Frederick II was aware of it. In mid-1756, he tried to gain guarantees that the gathering Russian and Austrian armies were aimed against Prussia, but none were given. He now realized that an invasion was imminent, with it most likely coming in early 1757. He decided not to wait. In August 1756, Prussia invaded Saxony, kicking off the Third Silesian War, which was, in turn, part of a much wider conflict known as the Seven Years' War. This gave the Austro-Russian coalition a diplomatic excuse to attack. They were joined by Saxony, whose participation wasn't yet formalized at the time but was expected, as well as Sweden, which dreamed of taking back Pomerania. On the other hand, only Portugal decided to side with Britain and Prussia, while the other less powerful Germanic states formed two opposing blocs, depending on their interests and positions.

When the war started, Prussia found itself fighting for survival. If the Austro-Russian coalition's plans were to come true, the Hohenzollerns would be left only with Brandenburg. Looking at the opposition forces, it seemed like Frederick had little chance to win. Unlike the two previous Silesian wars, this one wasn't a string of Prussian victories. Instead, in the sixteen major battles, only half were won by Frederick. However, each victory was enough to keep Prussia afloat. This played to his hand because, apart from Maria

Theresa, the other enemies weren't so upset at Frederick II. Thus, France remained mostly preoccupied with its Atlantic struggle against Britain. Its commitment was further tested when a Prussian force of twenty thousand inflicted a crushing defeat on a French-Austrian force twice that size at the Battle of Rossbach in November of 1757. It was actually the only direct confrontation between French and Prussian troops, but it was enough for the former to decide to become only a financial ally to the coalition beginning in March of 1758. At roughly the same time, Britain sent substantial economic aid to its ally, helping Frederick's war effort.

A contemporary painting of the Battle of Rossbach. Source:
https://commons.wikimedia.org

This mismatched battle record of Frederick's armies also proved that he wasn't an undefeatable military genius. Although he had a keen tactical mind, he also had his drawbacks. For example, in the Battle of Kunersdorf in August of 1759, Frederick showed his flawed comprehension of how the battle unfolded. He lost more than a third of his army in a decisive defeat against the Austro-Russian forces. Furthermore, some victories proved too costly to yield any actual gains. This can be seen in the Battle of Torgau in November 1760, when roughly fifty thousand Prussians defeated an Austrian army of the same size, with both sides losing some fifteen thousand men. It was a Pyrrhic victory in a strategic sense since Prussia gained little from it. However, it seemed that Frederick was capable of winning when it was necessary, and he had a stunning ability to recover from defeats and inflict crucial blows on his enemies. This was partially due to his military capabilities, which mostly stemmed from him keeping a cool head amidst a crisis, but also because the Prussian military was usually the better-trained force on the battlefield.

In the end, it seemed that time worked in Frederick's favor, though it may not have seemed like that at the time. As the war dragged on, with all nations suffering from exhaustion, Austria's allies started to flake. First, Russia withdrew from the war in early 1762 after a change on its throne. They were quickly followed by Sweden, who had no strength to fight the Prussians on their own and were too far away from the Habsburgs. By the December of that year, representatives from Saxony, Austria, and Prussia began their own negotiations. These were only hastened when France and Britain signed their own peace, with Saxony, Austria, and Prussia concluding their treaty on February 15th, 1763, at Hubertusburg Castle. Under its provisions, *status quo ante bellum* was reinforced, which had been Frederick's only real goal. In addition, Austria publicly denounced its claim on Silesia, and, in return, Frederick vowed to vote for Maria Theresa's son in the upcoming imperial elections.

The Third Silesian War is usually depicted as a Prussian victory. And, on most accounts, it was, as Frederick managed to hold on to his previous gains and repel a powerful coalition that wanted to dismember his state. However, it was a costly victory. In the simplest terms, it emptied the Prussian treasury. It was even costlier in terms of human lives. All the major battles left armies with thousands killed in action, with many more perishing from hunger, diseases, or succumbing to battle wounds along the way. According to some rough estimates, some 180,000 Prussian soldiers lost their lives in combat. Even worse, throughout the war, most Prussian territories were invaded by enemy forces. The occupation wasn't as traumatizing as during the Thirty Years' War, as the majority of troops were now more disciplined and supplied by their states, yet the local population still suffered. Invading armies extorted money and supplies, and there were also cases of war atrocities, such as pillaging, murder, and rape. These were mostly done by the irregular "light troops," which were filled with volunteers and were semi-autonomous auxiliary units of the main army.

If the direct violence wasn't enough, occupied lands also suffered from food shortages and, even worse, various epidemics that the armies brought with them. These diseases likely accounted for most of the civilian deaths. It is important to note that the Prussian armies brought the same misery to the enemy lands they occupied. That was just a part of war in the 18th century. It was mostly unavoidable, as armies were a burden even on their own territories. Nevertheless, when the civilian casualties are added up, Brandenburg-Prussia lost some 400,000 people during the war. That is roughly 10 percent of its population, a terrible blow to its demographics and, in turn, the economy. The loss of lives, coupled with the destruction and pillaging of the invaders, left many farms abandoned, and there was also a substantial amount of damaged property and infrastructure. Thus, these should also be accounted for when measuring the success of Prussia's participation in the Third Silesian War.

In the end, besides preserving its borders and losing hundreds of thousands of lives, Prussia also gained something its rulers had coveted for a long time. Its position as a great power was acknowledged by the other European nations, even though it was still not on the same level as, for example, France or Britain. Through the three wars for Silesia, Frederick finally accumulated enough recognition and glory for himself, the Prussian state, and the Hohenzollern dynasty.

Chapter 6 – From Glory to Humiliation

Despite what seemed like a magnificent victory against overwhelming odds, Frederick the Great wasn't ready to relax and enjoy the fruits of his conquests. Being the keen statesmen he was, the Prussian king was aware that Brandenburg-Prussia was devastated, in need of recuperation, and, most of all, not yet safe.

After 1763, Frederick turned toward rebuilding and repopulating his state. Like his predecessors, he lured immigrants to the depopulated regions, promising them lands to live and work on. He also financed the building of a canal system, which drained marshy lands previously unavailable for farming. In turn, the same canals would also ease up market integration and supply shipping. During his reign, the potato and turnip were introduced in Prussia as a new type of crop, ones better suited to combat famine. To this end, Frederick also reorganized the system of state grain magazines and began actively using the grain excise tax to influence the import of basic foods. With the latter, he first suspended the taxation of all grains in 1766, allowing for cheaper imports from Poland. Then, when the situation bettered, he introduced the excise tax on wheat, which was at the time used by better-situated classes. This way, taxation fell on those with enough money to pay them. In the case of the grain magazines, Frederick used them to release stored grains during times of famine, which was particularly important in 1771 and 1772 when there was a Europe-wide shortage.

A portrait of Frederick II from the 1780s. Source: https://commons.wikimedia.org

This showed that after the war, Frederick had at least the same amount of attention for social issues as for the military because the primary role of the magazine system was to hold supplies for the army. Similarly, the king also showed surprising care for his veterans. He set up an institution to care for invalids, provided monetary subsidies for poverty-stricken soldiers, and made low-wage jobs at the lowest levels of governmental posts available to those who fought for him and the state. It was his way of repaying those who had risked everything for him.

Apart from welfare, Frederick continued to rebuild and enlarge his army. He was aware that the security of all his gains rested upon the strength of the Prussian Army. His military had some 195,000 soldiers in the last years of his reign, making it officially the third-largest army in Europe, despite being the thirteenth state by population. This meant that roughly 3.4 percent of Prussians were serving. This led to the famous depiction of the Prussian monarchy being a military with a state rather than the other way around.

Nevertheless, Frederick never again committed his troops to any serious warfare. The only time they rode to combat was in the War of the Bavarian Succession. This came about when the Habsburgs tried to seize Bavaria after its ruling dynasty had died out. Prussia and Saxony opposed it, and in mid-1778, it escalated into a war. Frederick once again led his troops, invading Habsburg-held Bohemia; however, no major battle occurred as the two armies maneuvered around each other, succumbing mostly to famine and disease. Neither Frederick nor Maria Theresa, who was now a co-ruler with her son Joseph, wanted this to turn into another bloody conflict, so the war was concluded with a peace treaty in May of 1779. The deal was struck with the mediation of Russia and France. Bavaria was left to a side branch of its previous dynasty, while Austria gained a small territorial compensation along its border with Bavaria. In return, the Habsburgs recognized the Prussian claim on the duchies of Ansbach and Bayreuth, though their acquisition was to come some years later.

The War of the Bavarian Succession confirmed that the Holy Roman Empire was influenced by more than one king. It was no longer solely the Habsburgs' playground; they had to share authority with the Hohenzollerns. However, Frederick's crowning achievement in terms of diplomacy and power status had come a few years before. In the late 1760s, Russia was waging a successful war against the Ottomans. That caused concern in Austria, and it seemed that another major war was brewing on the horizon. The

Habsburgs were determined to maintain the perceived balance of power. Such a development was unfavorable for Frederick, as he had become a Russian ally in 1764. So, he turned toward diplomacy, an action that showcased that Frederick's political skills were equal to his military capabilities. He refocused both Austria's and Russia's attention on Poland, which was, at the time, still officially the Polish-Lithuanian Commonwealth. For some time, Poland had been on a downward spiral on a political, military, and economic level. It lost its "major power" status, slowly becoming dependent on other nations, most notably Russia. Because of that, it was the perfect prey.

Frederick, with the help of his brother Henry (Heinrich), entered negotiations with Vienna and Saint Petersburg. He proposed that the three states divide Poland, preserving the balance of power, instead of waging another war over the lands that Russia would take from the Turks. The talks lasted for roughly two years, between 1770 to 1772, until the three sides finally agreed on the so-called First Partition of Poland. However, even before they ended, all three sides began occupying their desired territories. Austria gained the most populated share in the partition, occupying the provinces of Galicia and Lodomeria. Russia took a slightly larger territory, which was mostly located in present-day Belarus and Latvia, though it had a lesser population. Prussia gained the least from the partition, at least in raw numbers. Its territorial gains represented 5 percent of the commonwealth, compared with Russia's 12.7 percent and Austria's 11.8 percent. In it were some 600,000 new subjects, compared with 1.3 million for Russia and 2.6 for Austria. However, it was by far the most important gain strategically, as it consisted of so-called Royal Prussia, without Danzig (Gdańsk), along with two additional border districts. These lands became known as West Prussia, finally connecting East Prussia with Brandenburg. Furthermore, this territory held important economic value because of its ports and developed trade connections.

Taking over Royal Prussia and uniting the entirety of Prussian lands under the Hohenzollern rule allowed for a less palpable but no less important act. In 1772, Frederick II changed his title from "King in Prussia" to the more common monarchical term of "King of Prussia." This was done because, by then, neither Poland nor the Habsburgs could object. It goes without saying that Frederick did this without consulting the emperor in Vienna. He also arranged it so that the titles Duke of Prussia and Elector of Brandenburg were attached to the kingly title. This was purely a display of the sovereignty and autonomy of the newly strengthened Prussian state and its position as being an equal to other European powers. It also helped speed up the process of the "Prussianization" of the Hohenzollern state. As the 18th century drew closer to its final years, contemporaries began avoiding using cumbersome "Brandenburg-Prussia" in favor of "Prussian lands" or simply "Prussia," though the latter was officially accepted only in the early years of the 19th century.

Map of Europe in 1786, with all Prussian gains during Frederick's reign.
Source: https://commons.wikimedia.org

Thus, the lands of the Hohenzollerns began shedding their dualistic nature during Frederick II's reign. From his rule and onward, it would be historically correct to call his lands Prussia. However, all that was merely a titular matter. More important was the fact that his rule also worked to unify the people. Like in many other European nations at the time, a sense of patriotism began to arise, a precursor to the nationalism of the 19th century. In Prussia, it was largely centered around the allegiance to the king, particularly Frederick the Great. Without much aid from his personal actions, a cult of personality was born, and it only grew after his death. Nevertheless, through his personality, his subjects began creating a shared identity under the umbrella term "Prussians," through which people of all classes and backgrounds shared a unifying factor. The loyalty to the king then transitioned to loyalty toward the state, as the two were somewhat synonymous at the time. One's love and devotion to the state were only increased through the wars and joint struggles, helping to create the ideals of dying for one's nation. Of course, like with any feelings of that kind, patriotism created resentment and dislike for other nations. In Prussia's case, it was most notably the Russians and French. However, there was a similar separation between "us and them" with other Germanic states, like Austria, Franconia, or Bavaria.

As for other internal policies, Frederick II acted as an enlightened absolutist, somewhat of a combination of his father and his grandfather. He continued to modernize the state's administration, though not at the same pace as during Frederick William's reign. The long periods of war hampered such developments, but after 1763, there were some actions in that direction. Despite the disdain Frederick II held for his father, he eventually went a step beyond, despite claiming that the king was only the first servant of the state. During his long rule, the entire bureaucratic system revolved around him, and he somewhat disregarded ministers and directories. Every major decision came from the king, and he often worked directly with provincial officials, which led to a certain level of decentralization. According to his idea of "allegiance to the state," Frederick always put the well-being of the state before his personal gains, actively working to protect and develop the industry and economy. Yet, Frederick's absolutism only grew in his later years, prompting Voltaire to denounce him as an enlightened philosopher.

Nevertheless, Frederick retained some central ideas of the Enlightenment. Most notable was his willingness to invest in the arts and science, reopening some of the universities his father had closed. He invited philosophers, artists, and other intellectuals to come to Prussia, hoping to elevate it culturally. Furthermore, the king erected numerous public buildings connected with culture, like the Berlin Opera or Royal Library, both of which are still standing in the German capital. Thanks to Frederick's religious skepticism, he also promoted religious tolerance to a much larger degree than in any of the surrounding states. However, he retained some amount of prejudice, especially toward the Jews, but that never led to any persecutions. In fact, he worked hard to integrate them into the emerging Prussian society. Further developing upon the ideas of the Enlightenment, Frederick granted his subjects a substantial amount of freedom of speech, and he also worked on reforming the judicial system to abolish torture and death sentences. This led to the reorganization of the courts and laws, and he created a unified code of law that would serve the state before anything. However, the General Prussian Code of Law was finished in 1794, several years after his death. All of those facts confirm that, despite his absolutism, Frederick the Great remained faithful to some ideals of the Enlightenment until his final days in 1786.

Frederick II was succeeded by his nephew, Frederick William II, the son of his younger brother, Prince Augustus William (August Wilhelm), who died in 1758. The new king was similar to his illustrious uncle. Frederick William was also quite interested in the arts and played the cello, and he showed signs of a capable intellect.

However, he had large shoes to fill, and he lacked any proper training in state affairs. Making matters worse for Frederick William II was the fact that Europe was about to enter one of its most turbulent periods, with the French Revolution and the subsequent Napoleonic Wars. In such trying times, Frederick William's average capabilities simply weren't enough. Trying to prove his worth in comparison to Frederick II, the new king tried to relax taxation and burdens on the people, gaining some popularity while losing economic stability. Furthermore, though he continued to expand the Prussian Army, he chose not to oversee it personally, leaving it under the control of the Supreme College of War. This gave an impetus to the degradation of Prussian military might, as the increase in quantity was paired with a drop in the quality of the troops.

A portrait of Frederick William II. Source: https://commons.wikimedia.org

Despite that, it seems that Frederick William tried to maintain the status of Prussia being a major European power. First, in 1787, he intervened in the Netherlands, supporting the ruling party in a civil war. It was a low-key adventure that brought only expenses without any palpable gains. Then, his focus turned southward to the Habsburgs, who began a new war against the Ottoman Empire in the Balkans. Since the Turks were already entangled in a conflict against the Russians, the Habsburgs were in a very good position to acquire new territories and restore their dominant position in the Germanic world. Of course, Frederick William wasn't keen on seeing this; thus, when a chain of revolts erupted across the Habsburg Monarchy in 1789, the Prussians were quick to encourage them and even entered into some talks of assisting them. At roughly the same time, France was engulfed in the first wave of its revolution. While most European monarchies condemned it, Prussia remained neutral, verging on supporting it. This was done because there was some liberal support for revolutionaries rebelling against "despotism" in Paris but more because it was disrupting the Habsburg-Bourbon alliance. Austria was losing its major ally, making Prussia's position stronger than before.

At that moment, Prussia's foreign policy began to change. First, the Austrian ruler approached Frederick William. The Habsburg emperor was wary of the possibility of a Prussian-backed insurrection in Hungary, so he proposed to find common ground. In mid-1790, after a long negotiation, the two sides agreed that Austria would abandon all the new lands taken from the Ottomans, while the Prussians would stop encouraging rebellions in the Habsburg lands. It marked the start of Austro-Prussian rapprochement, as the two slowly began turning against the French revolutionaries, who were becoming more and more radical. By mid-1791, the Habsburgs and the Hohenzollerns had become allies, announcing their support for the Bourbon king. The allies then continued to iron out details of their actions against the revolutionaries, which was accompanied by the usual political negotiations on gains and territories. However, even before they could arrange a course of action, revolutionary France declared war on Austria in early 1792. By the summer, the joint Austro-Prussian forces were marching toward France.

Like in the previous similar offensives, the Germanic forces had a rough time coordinating and executing their plans on the western periphery of the Holy Roman Empire. Their effectiveness was only lowered by the resentment of local Frenchmen. The joint force managed to take control of the border fortresses of Longwy and Verdun as they slowly moved toward Paris. Then, in late September, the invading Austro-Prussian force encountered its first real opposition from the revolutionaries at Valmy. Two armies of roughly equal size, around thirty-five thousand men each, faced off in what technically ended in a tactical draw. The two sides exchanged artillery fire before the Germanic forces withdrew. The reason why is unclear, but it seems that the Prussians weren't keen on fighting against well-positioned French defenders. It is possible that they were saving their troops for the new troubles brewing east in Poland. Regardless, the revolutionaries felt the wind in their sails when the joint force retreated. After the Battle of Valmy, Prussia's participation in the war against France was minimal, although some of their troops continued to participate.

Prussia's primary concern was once again Poland, where a new government had tried to enact reforms and stabilize the country. The possibility of a renewed Polish-Lithuanian Commonwealth was unacceptable both to the Prussians and Russians. With Prussian forces tied up in France, Russia intervened in Poland. Of course, such actions alarmed Frederick William II, as it opened the possibility of Russian expansion and posed a threat to Prussia. Initially, he thought about supporting the Poles, but he found it much easier to find common ground with the Russians. After some discussion, by early 1793, the two nations had agreed to another partition of Poland. The Russians took almost half of the Polish territories in the east, some 97,000 square miles (250,000 square kilometers), while the Prussian crown was awarded 22,000 square miles (58,000 square kilometers) for not acting against them. The Habsburgs didn't react since they were too preoccupied with the French; in addition, part of their alliance with Frederick William stipulated support for further expansion in Poland. Thus, Prussia gained the cities of Danzig (Gdańsk) and Thorn (Toruń), which were important economic centers. Plus, it was more land than the king had even hoped for.

Merely a year after the Second Partition of Poland, the Poles rebelled against the stationed Russian troops and the Polish nobility loyal to Saint Petersburg. They were partly inspired by the French Revolution. This time, the Prussians were the first to act, yet their forces were stretched too thinly. The Russians and Austrians soon came to help, leaving the Poles without a chance. By late 1794, they had been crushed. The only thing that was left was for the three victorious nations to agree upon the third and final partition of Poland. Realizing that new territories would bring a further strain on the state administration and that the Prussian treasury and army were exhausted, Frederick William struck a peace treaty with the French in early 1795. Since Prussia was the first of the monarchies to yield to the French Republic, which was established after Valmy, it was seen as a betrayal and an act of cowardice from its former allies. Nevertheless, by October of that year, through negotiations with Russia and Austria, Prussia secured around 21,000 square miles (55,000 square kilometers) of Polish territories around Warsaw.

Map of the three partitions of Poland, with Prussian gains colored in blue.
Source: https://commons.wikimedia.org

However, from then on, Prussia was left isolated and alone. Frederick William II managed to ally and then abandon all the major European powers during his reign, making his messy duplicitous diplomacy unwelcomed in most courts. The Austrians released propaganda attacks, calling the Prussians cowards and wicked, with similar tones resonating with later historians. Yet, when looking at reality, for Prussia, it seemed like the best course of action. The new lands were rebellious, and the Prussian Army and administration were overextended and exhausted. Fighting against France, which, at the time, had shown little malice toward Prussia, seemed disruptive and unnecessary. The separate peace, at least on paper, also created a neutral zone in the northern Germanic lands and refocused the French on Prussia's traditional adversary: the Habsburgs. From that perspective, a separate peace seemed reasonable, yet its consequences showed that Frederick William lacked the foresight most of his predecessors had.

Besides being left without any allies and friends, Prussia's demeanor in dealing with France signaled that Berlin was apathetic toward the fate of the Holy Roman Empire, creating the final tear in its institutional fabric. In trying to preserve peace and increase his power, Frederick William II tried to influence other Germanic princes to follow suit. Soon, even the Habsburgs adopted such a stance, focusing on their own personal gains more than on the fate of the empire. An additional problem for Prussia was that with the destruction of Poland, it lost its only buffer state against the Russians in the east. Its future became intrinsically tied with its more powerful eastern neighbor. Nevertheless, for a short while, it seemed that Prussia might be well off. As one of the least impressive rulers in the Hohenzollern dynasty from the 16th century onward, Frederick William still managed to enlarge his state a third and increase the number of his subjects from 5.5 to 8.7 million. He passed away in late 1797 before he could see the full effects of his ill-advised diplomacy.

Frederick William II was succeeded by his son, twenty-seven-year-old Frederick William III. He was quite introverted and shy, and he was somewhat melancholic but also pious and honest. Like most of his Hohenzollern predecessors, he had a troubled relationship with his father. Frederick William III felt neglected by his father. He was raised by tutors and educators and thus suffered from an inferiority complex his entire life. The new king also felt disgusted by his father's court, which was filled with cliques and intrigues, as well as adultery. In contrast, Frederick William III was devoutly faithful to his wife, and he worked on restoring the morality of the Prussian court and cutting expenses. However, he also exhibited an unnatural distrust of his ministers and delegates. The young king wanted to personally dominate state affairs, but he lacked the capabilities of his great-uncle Frederick II. For this reason, his reign lacked consistency and efficiency.

Like his father, the new king was an average ruler who was thrown into one of the most chaotic periods of European history. Initially, Frederick William tried to remain neutral, staying out of the Second and Third coalition wars against France. In the process, he was willing to make territorial trades within the boundaries of the crumbling Holy Roman Empire, as did other princes and even the Habsburg Empire. In those dealings, Frederick William III relinquished some 1,000 square miles (2,600 square kilometers) and about 125,000 subjects in return for 5,000 square miles (13,000 square kilometers) and almost 500,000 people. Thus, the empire's number of constituent states dwindled while the Habsburgs continued their struggles against the French, who were slowly regressing into a monarchy under Napoleon Bonaparte. That tendency was confirmed in 1804 when Napoleon was proclaimed an emperor. This was coupled with the Habsburg emperor crowning himself as the "Emperor of Austria." After the War of the Third Coalition was over, the Holy Roman Empire was dissolved. In its place, Napoleon created the Confederation of the Rhine, an alliance of French client states that excluded both Prussia and Austria.

Paintings of Frederick William III (top) and Napoleon Bonaparte (bottom).
Source: https://commons.wikimedia.org

This was the final sign that Prussia wasn't going to be safe solely through the ink on paper. In the years that led up to the creation of the confederation, it became clear that, for the French, especially Napoleon, Prussia was merely a second-rate power. The supposed Prussian domination over northern Germanic states that had existed due to a 1795 treaty was circumvented, as France did as it pleased. Its occupation of British-held Hanover in 1803 is probably the best example of this. Furthermore, not only was northern Germanic neutrality ignored but also Prussian noninvolvement. Both the Russian and the French armies crossed Prussian territory when they needed. By 1805, Frederick William III found himself in a precarious position. He needed to choose a side or be swallowed. He initially tried to ally himself with Russia and Austria in the Third War of the Coalition, but both empires yielded to France before he could join. Thus, Prussia had to realign with the French, becoming more of a client state than an equal partner.

When Napoleon created a new confederation in place of the Holy Roman Empire, he finally forced Frederick William to act. It excluded Prussia from the Germanic world while at the same time consolidating its client states and giving them higher titles. None of these actions were done with any consideration to the king of Prussia, which means he was dealt with like any other Germanic client prince. For the Prussians, it was all too much, even the pro-French in the court, prompting Frederick William to seek an alliance with Russia and Saxony. At the time, Sweden and Britain were already fighting France, making the bones of the Fourth Coalition, while the Austrians recovered from their previous defeat. Prussian involvement began with an ultimatum to Napoleon to withdraw behind the Rhine or face the consequences. It was sent on October 1st, 1806, giving the French a week to comply. This led to Prussia's declaration of war a day after the deadline since, as expected, Napoleon dismissed the ultimatum.

The French Army was already stationed in the southern Germanic states, so it marched quicker than the Prussians expected. Napoleon's army brushed through the initial Prussian defenses on its borders toward Bavaria as it marched to Berlin. By October 14th, 1806, the main Prussian forces met the French in a double Battle of Jena–Auerstedt in modern-day Thuringia. At Jena, the two sides had roughly equal troop numbers, around fifty thousand to fifty-five thousand men each. At Auerstedt, a similarly sized Prussian Army faced a French regiment that was twice as small. Despite that, both battles ended in a crushing Prussian defeat. The Prussian Army lost some forty thousand men, while many others surrendered. The entire military force built by Frederick William's predecessors during the 18th century had been swept away in a single blow. The royal court fled to East Prussia and the safety of Königsberg, while the rest of the kingdom was overrun by the end of the month. It was only then that the Russians managed to roll into the conflict from the east.

A later illustration of the retreating Prussian soldiers after Jena–Auerstedt.
Source: https://commons.wikimedia.org

During the next several months, Frederick William and Napoleon tried to negotiate a peace treaty. However, Napoleon seemed hell-bent on humiliating the Prussians, despite showing immense respect to Frederick the Great while in occupied Berlin. All the while, the Prussians hoped that Imperial Russia could deliver a devastating blow to the French Army. In the end, despite some success, the Russian tsar lost the will to fight and agreed on peace negotiations in July of 1807. The two emperors met near Tilsit (modern-day Sovetsk) on a raft in the middle of the Niemen River, with Frederick William being left as an observer on the banks, only expanding on his humiliation. France and Russia concluded the Treaty of Tilsit, and Prussia had to accept the terms without negotiations. Napoleon reduced Prussia in half, both in size and population. Almost all the territories gained in the Second and Third Partitions of Poland were lost to a new Franco-Polish satellite state. At the same time, all Prussian possessions west of the Elbe River were given to French allies. Furthermore, Prussia had to pay an immense indemnity, some fifteen years' worth of its pre-1806 annual state revenue. The Prussian Army was reduced to merely forty-two thousand men. Finally, what was left of Prussia had to house and feed some 150,000 French occupation soldiers.

In the end, the Treaty of Tilsit finally reduced Prussia to the same level as all the other Germanic principalities, making it just another client state among many across Europe. The Hohenzollern monarchy hadn't found itself in such a position since the Thirty Years' War in the early 17th century, and it would leave a similar traumatic mark on the people's consciousness.

Chapter 7 – Recuperation through Reforms

With a single blow, Napoleon and the French had more or less set Prussia back almost a century, if not more. Its territory was reduced, its diplomatic position diminished, its military crippled, and its economy paralyzed. Prussia's very existence was threatened, as it seems the French emperor had only scorn for the Prussians. The Hohenzollern monarchy was spared because Napoleon wasn't sure what to do with it, while the Russians had advocated for its survival during the peace negotiations.

Before Frederick William III and the Prussian state stood two paths. One was to accept their fate and hope for a better tomorrow, or they could work on bettering their situation. The king and, more importantly, his closest advisors chose the latter, prompting a series of reforms in the next several years. Those changes were mainly led by Heinrich Friedrich Karl vom Stein and Karl August von Hardenberg, two experienced statesmen whose careers dated to the era of Frederick the Great. Their reforms are often represented merely as an answer to the Prussian state crisis after Tilsit; however, this debacle only gave impetus to changes that were slowly brewing behind the political scene. Their true roots were in the Prussian

Enlightenment, which had been so wholeheartedly supported by Frederick II. During his long reign, the great Prussian king championed education, debate, free thoughts, and other expressions of culture. He worked hard on gathering some of the most notable thinkers in the Germanic lands and wider. It should suffice to say that one of the most famous philosophers of all time, Immanuel Kant, was one of many individuals who thrived in the fertile soils of the Prussian Enlightenment.

The Enlightenment, though, was somewhat stifled during Frederick William II's reign. He was more in line with traditional absolutism than his uncle's enlightened form. Nevertheless, many of the ideas and thoughts survived, and some even passed to his son, Frederick William III. His role is sometimes diminished in the reforms enacted by his bureaucrats, yet it was the monarch who gave them their position and the support needed to carry through with these much-needed changes. This was crucial, especially since most of the nobles seemed to be against any alterations to the existing system. Even more importantly, the king himself dabbled in reform ideas, inquiring about transforming the prison system and state finances before the defeat. He backed down partially because he found stern resistance among his officials but even more so due to his feeling of inadequacy. His lack of confidence was caused by the fact that his father didn't prepare him for the role of the monarch, although the king also had to contend with his shy personality. Nevertheless, this crushing defeat turned the atmosphere in the court around, and once again, Prussia was fertile ground for reforms.

Before delving into the details of Prussia's reforms, it is vital to note that they began under Stein's tutelage. He was the king's chancellor, but he became a thorn in Napoleon's side in late 1808, when French spies intercepted Stein's letter that was filled with anti-French sentiment. He pressured Frederick William to dismiss Stein, and for a while, the Prussian king resisted. Yet, in 1809, Stein fled into exile, and his work was continued by Hardenberg, with whom Stein worked closely while in office. Hardenberg not only continued but also expanded on Stein's ideas in the following years, though not always to Stein's approval. It is worth noting that these reforms were not solely Stein's and Hardenberg's fruits of labor. They worked with a number of scholars, economists, and statesmen to achieve all that they planned and wanted. Among them were Heinrich Theodor von Schön, Wilhelm von Humboldt, and Carl von Clausewitz, just to mention a few. In reality, the changes were brought about by the cooperation of a group of like-minded people under the king's service and support.

Paintings of Stein (top) and Hardenberg (bottom). Source:
https://commons.wikimedia.org

The reformers' first task was streamlining the government. Until that point, state bureaucracy was stuck in the old double-structured governance, with overlapping jurisdictions between the central and local administrations. The first order of business was to replace the old General Directory with the Ministry of State (*Staatsministerium*). It consisted of five ministers, whose authority no longer combined specified tasks and territories; instead, the ministers were given a single governmental field. Thus, there were ministries of the interior, foreign affairs, finance, war, and justice. The initial collegial nature of the Ministry of State was changed with the introduction of the state chancellor (*Staatskanzler*) in 1810, a position first awarded to Hardenberg. At a local level, Prussia finally created an integrated provincial system, abolishing the last traces of the historical ducal administration. Every province had its own local governmental body with a ministerial division similar to the central administration and a high commissioner (*Oberpräsident*), who was directly subordinate to and represented the Ministry of State. Provinces were administratively subdivided into districts and townships while also given locally elected diets to increase the idea of self-rule.

Such regional autonomy seemed to be one of the goals of the reformers, as Stein had also reorganized towns in a similar manner. He put all cities under the same administrative bureaucracy with identical rights and obligations. Then, he proceeded to return governing rights from the central to the local administration while also forcing the citizens to participate in them. In 1810, reformers also tried to uplift the idea of self-governance on a state level, as Hardenberg formed the Council of the State (*Staatsrat*), which was, in a way, the forerunner of the National Assembly. It was supposed to prevent the state from regressing into full absolutism, as the council would have a say on laws and administrative procedures. However, the council never managed to catch on, and Prussia remained without a parliament until 1848.

Frederick William wasn't merely a passive bystander when it came to the bureaucratization of the state. At some point, Stein wanted to curb the crown's authority by making a royal decree valid only if it had the signatures of all five ministers. Of course, the king refused, and Stein was, for a short while, in Frederick William's bad graces. Regardless, the new system unshackled the state from absolutism and its reliance on the capabilities of a single person and also made governing more efficient across the entire nation.

The second task set before the reformers was streamlining the economy, more precisely, state revenue. This was, in a way, the reformers' primary goal for these changes, as paying indemnity to France was the only thing keeping Prussia alive. Thus, Hardenberg worked on tax standardization, replacing a wide variety of local and minor taxes with statewide uniform taxation. Furthermore, excise taxes were expanded beyond just cities, though on a lesser variety of products, like luxury goods, alcohol, and tobacco. Taxation on the commercial and industrial sectors was also reorganized, with a progressively spread-out trade tax. New taxes were also added on income and wealth, but these were only marginally successful, as the nobility found a way to circumvent property taxes, leading to a class tax, an intermediate between the poll and income taxes. Apart from taxation, customs duties were also reformed, though this was finished only after Napoleon was defeated. Internal tariffs were lifted, as well as export bans set up by Frederick II. The import duties were heavier on products that competed with the local industrial economy, which was still too weak to fend for itself. Transport duties were also put in place, adding additional state revenue.

Overall, the reforms tried to spur the economy with more progressive taxation, with the intention to put the majority of the burden on the nobles and the rich. Such plans failed, most notably in the idea of equal taxation for all citizens, something the nobles protested. In that aspect, the reformers found themselves in a struggle with the fading aristocracy. However, for the nobility, the most troublesome issue was the termination of serfdom, which was carried out in the October Edict of 1807, followed by several more ordinances and edicts for further clarification and regulation. These included the problems of corvée labor, which had initially remained in place, as well as the issues of land ownership and reimbursement. Yet, the nobility quickly turned around and accepted the new system, as they realized they gained more through this new land distribution while the peasants gained little. Most of the peasants were unable to pay for their lands; thus, it would revert to the nobles, who would then hire the peasants as cheap labor. In the end, the agricultural reforms failed to make society equal, to some extent even furthering the concentration of wealth, but it did increase production output by modernizing the system.

The October Edict of 1807 (top) and Humboldt (bottom). Source: https://commons.wikimedia.org

The more important byproduct of the abolition of serfdom was the peasants' freedom. After 1807, they were allowed to move and to do as they pleased with their lives, without being bound to the land or their masters. This allowed for a much-needed influx of laborers to the cities, giving a spark to Prussia's industrial economy. Luckily, the reformers were aware of the importance of industries. Thus, they enacted a policy of the freedom of industry, where the market dictated how it would develop. Guilds lost their monopolies, and their membership became voluntary. Anyone could set up an industrial workshop, wherever and however they pleased, as long as they acquired a state license. Furthermore, legal differences between the cities and the countryside in terms of industrial endeavors were eradicated. The basic principles of industry were now free competition and free professional choice. The only exception was mining, which remained a state monopoly until the 1860s. The liberalization of industry gave way to its rise, which, in turn, became the foundation of Prussia's economic rebirth.

An important part of the reforms was also the change in Prussian society. This was partially achieved by widening citizenship status. That designation wasn't limited solely to members of privileged township strata, as it also included all people who owned a house, including, in rare cases, single women. Thus, voting rights in cities were wider than ever before, though still limited to the local government levels. This was followed by the further inclusion of Jews in Prussian society. The Edict of Emancipation of 1812 gave them the same liberties, rights, and duties as all other citizens. However, Jews could still not achieve military ranks and high positions in the state administration. Of course, this was at least partially caused by economic necessity, as Jews had been previously banned from certain professions. However, this process was more a result of the Enlightenment, during which time Jewish society emerged out of isolation and came in contact with the Prussian elite. In fact, Hardenberg was a frequent guest in Jewish homes and counted many of them as his friends. Yet, full Jewish integration wasn't immediately achieved, as many Prussians held on to their misconceptions and prejudices against them.

Educational reforms were also part of the societal changes, and they were mostly headed by Humboldt. Like with the other reforms, the initial issue was the standardization of education. A wide variety of private, religious, and municipal educational institutions were molded into a three-tier schooling system, starting from People's Schools (*Volksschule*), the elementary level, after which came gymnasiums, which were then followed by universities. The main goal was to no longer merely teach specific subjects but instead turn children into people capable of learning for themselves. Humboldt then proceeded to open schools for teachers, helping the standardization of this system, which was completely under state control. Education was compulsory, and the state issued all curriculums and created exams. Furthermore, any civil service position required a certain level of education, and performance replaced one's social origin as the main qualifier. Apart from that, Humboldt's reforms also brought humanistic ideas to education, allowing schools to depart from the purely utilitarian form of the Enlightenment. He also envisioned the autonomy of universities and academia. The state and politics should be absent from them, leaving universities to pursue higher intellectual goals according to the scientific method. Thus, Humboldt's educational system, in theory, produced educated and interested citizens who were capable of self-governance.

Of course, there were others who deemed that, in certain areas, Humboldt was wrong. His humanistic individualism was often attacked the most. Many thought that education should be used to mold people for the needs of the state and, even more, the nation, especially as a form of resistance against Napoleon. However, in that aspect, military reforms were more important. Like other changes, these were done as a collaboration of several officers, with Clausewitz being probably the most famous of the group, even though he was the youngest. One of their principal complaints was that the Prussian Army lacked motivation and that patriotism should be the main motivator for soldiers. In turn, service in the army should instill nationalistic feelings in the soldiers, creating a loop, as these thoughts would then be passed to their sons and neighbors. This was only furthered by reorganizing the army to treat its soldiers better, more like people than simple objects. The most severe physical punishments were abolished, and additional loyalty was also created by opening officer ranks to the non-nobility and basing promotions more on merit than on one's background.

Apart from rekindling the people's morale, the army went through important restructuring, similar to the governmental organization, making it much more streamlined. Additionally, the Ministry of War acted as a precursor to the Chief of Staff, and the army modernized both its equipment and training, creating more mobile and flexible units. The existing officer corps was purged, and tactics were updated. Finally, compulsory universal conscription was enacted, making all grown male adults viable for service if needed. This replaced the old system, which had been degraded even during Frederick II's reign into a bunch of foreign mercenaries serving the Prussian crown. Furthermore, a system of local militia was set up in 1813, creating the first seeds of the later *Landwehr*. It was supposed to be used solely for defending Prussian soil, and it wasn't part of the regular army, but later reforms would change that. The military reformers also found a way to train new soldiers while abiding by the Treaty of Tilsit. They rotated them so that there were never more than forty-two thousand active soldiers at a time.

Overall, the entire state was preparing to stand up to Napoleon. The military changes were aimed at equalizing the odds on the battlefield, the economic reforms gave strength to the home front while also buying time by paying the indemnity, and the new administration made it all better organized. Least of all, reforms brought a new sense of unity and patriotic feelings to the Prussians.

Despite that, Frederick William III was cautious about provoking the French. While the reforms were still ongoing, there were several mentions of rebellions and rejoining the war against Napoleon, yet the king decided not to act. Many in his court urged him to do something since the humiliating feeling of being under France's boot only accumulated. Nevertheless, Frederick William was aware that if Prussia stood up too soon, it might perish. Thus, years passed while resentment grew. It culminated in 1812 when Napoleon forced Berlin into a military treaty against Russia. Prussia was to open up its forts and quarter the French Grand Army (La Grande Armée) on its way east, as well as add twelve thousand Prussian soldiers to the cause. For some, like Clausewitz, that was too much, and a number of military officers defected to the Russian tsar, where they met up with the already exiled Stein.

Quartering some 300,000 men of the Grand Army rekindled the memory of the Thirty Years' War and the destruction caused by foreign armies. It also showcased that even the new Prussian system wasn't able to effectively house and feed such a mass. Nevertheless, the Prussian king stood silently. Rebellious emotions flared when the first news of French defeats near Moscow reached Prussia, yet Frederick William was still unsure if he should act. During December 1812, he remained inactive, but his subordinates began deciding instead of him. First, Clausewitz managed to persuade the Prussian part of the Grand Army to join the Russian cause and cease to assist the French retreat. Throughout January, the Prussian government slowly distanced itself from France, and the king fled from Berlin. Then, in early February 1813, Stein entered East Prussia, which basically ceased to heed Berlin and prepared for war against Napoleon. The spirit of insurrection spread across the remainder of Prussian lands, and in late February, Frederick William finally decided to side with the Russian Empire. In early March, he declared war and called upon his people for support in the struggle.

Early spring was mostly spent on preparations by both sides, with the first major combat occurring in May. These ended in French tactical victories, but they were paid for in a large number of casualties on both sides. A short armistice was agreed upon in June, allowing for some respite. By that time, Britain, Sweden, and Austria decided to officially join the new coalition. The latter two contributed armies, while Britain gave much-needed monetary subsidies. In August, the armistice ended, and hostilities resumed. Napoleon managed to gather more than 400,000 men, but many lacked proper training. Against them stood a coalition army of some 500,000 soldiers, around half of which were Prussians. The military reforms allowed Prussia to enlist 6 percent of its total population, meaning it had the largest army amongst the allies, despite its predicaments. It's vital to mention this was only the German front, as the Napoleonic Wars were fought across Europe and the world. Once the fighting resumed, battles were fought with mixed results. Several minor coalition victories were annulled by a single major French victory. Nevertheless, the Grand Army was slowly losing its footing, and Napoleon needed a decisive triumph.

He was unable to separate the allied army to defeat it, slowly maneuvering into a dead-end. The French were unable to retreat anymore, and Napoleon decided to accept a full-on battle at Leipzig. The two sides clashed in what amounted to be the largest battle of the war. It became known as the Battle of the Nations, with some 600,000 soldiers coming from France, various Germanic states (including Prussia), Russia, Sweden, Austria and all of its Hungarian and Balkan territories, Poland, and Italy. There was even a single British brigade present. At the height of the clash, the French had some 225,000 men against some 380,000 coalition soldiers, leaving them at a disadvantage. Nevertheless, the battle lasted from October 16th to October 19th, 1813, but it concluded with a decisive French defeat. Napoleon lost some seventy-three thousand men, while the coalition had some fifty-four thousand casualties, out of which sixteen thousand were Prussians. In the end, the Grand Army was forced to retreat to France, while most of Napoleon's Germanic allies abandoned him. His armies and supporters on other fronts were also losing, yet he refused a generous peace treaty sent by the allies, most notably the Austrians, who wanted to preserve a strong France as a balance to Russia.

A painting of the Battle of Leipzig. Source: https://commons.wikimedia.org

By late 1813 and early 1814, the coalition forces had entered France. Napoleon managed to achieve some smaller victories, but he no longer had an army capable of full-on resistance to numerically superior allies. The war ended in April 1814 when the French Senate deposed him. The deposed emperor was exiled, and the Bourbons were restored in Paris. By the autumn of 1814, the major powers, including defeated France, gathered at the Congress of Vienna to resolve the territorial and political issues left by the wars. However, in March 1815, Napoleon managed to return to France and gathered some loyal veterans in an attempt to win his throne back. Impressively, he gathered more than 250,000 soldiers, but he faced three to four times as many allied forces. In the end, Napoleon's final defeat came at Waterloo, Belgium. His 70,000 men stood against some 170,000 allied soldiers. Here, a crucial role was played by the fifty thousand Prussians under General Gebhard Leberecht von Blücher, who saved the British from collapsing and allowed the Duke of Wellington to turn the battle around. For that, Blücher was awarded an honorary doctorate from Oxford. In the end, Napoleon was defeated once and for all, and the Prussians proved their mettle as they slowly rebuilt their military reputation.

While the last coalition dealt with Napoleon's attempt of resurgence, the Congress of Vienna continued. It gathered some two hundred diplomats and statesmen of all European nations, including representatives of Bourbon France. However, the future of Europe was more or less forged by five major powers: Britain, Russia, Austria, Prussia, and France, despite its defeat. For Prussia, which was represented by Hardenberg and Humboldt, it was recognition. However, the Congress of Vienna showed that the other major powers didn't fully consider Prussia to be an equal member. Its representatives didn't acquire the gains as they were instructed, instead depending on agreements of other powers. Their main goal was to annex Saxony; however, the politics of the greater powers interfered. Prussia was given some 60 percent of its territory back; instead of receiving the rest, it gained the Duchy of Posen in Poland to block Russian expansion. The rest of the Polish territories gained in the Second and Third Partitions of Poland were willingly ceded to Russia even before the congress. Prussia also regained its western part, while Britain advocated for its further expansion in the Rhineland in an attempt to control France in the future.

The Prussian diplomacy defeat was even more pronounced when the question of the Germanic future arose. Prussia advocated a strong, dually centralized entity under a shared Austro-Prussian hegemony; in a way, it would be a reformed Holy Roman Empire in accordance with new levels of power and influence. However, Austria wanted a loosely tied union of free states, with a singular centralized body that was nothing more than a constant assembly of diplomatic representatives. In the end, the Austrian plan won, and the German Confederation was created. It encompassed thirty-eight Germanic states, though not all the Austrian and Prussian territories were part of it. For the latter, Posen and West and East Prussia remained outside of the confederation. Nevertheless, even in the newly formed confederation, there was a clear sense of dualism between Berlin and Vienna.

In the end, despite nearing something of a diplomatic failure at the Congress of Vienna, Prussia was left on solid ground. It had acquired significant territories, and the Hohenzollerns, for the first time, held more Germanic lands than their traditional Habsburgian foes. Their old competition was destined to flare once again.

Chapter 8 – Expanding Dominion over the Germanic World

The French Revolution and the subsequent Napoleonic Wars sent shockwaves across Europe. Entire political and social systems were uprooted across the continent. After a rather turbulent decade, Prussia, returning once again from the brink of destruction, found itself with something of a fresh start.

In geopolitical terms, it seems that Prussia's main preoccupation was ensuring its supremacy in the German Confederation, which essentially was a substitute for Prussia's previous disregard of the Holy Roman Empire. This subsequently made Austria its main political opponent. Its ministers focused mostly on two major questions: the joint security of the Germanic states and economic cooperation. The latter was done through the creation of the German Customs Union (*Zollverein*) in 1834, which incorporated almost all the Germanic states except for Austria. The whole process was slow, and Prussian politicians weren't initially in favor of such plans. It only began actualizing in 1827 when Prussia arranged for a customs agreement with Hesse, then slowly lured, blackmailed, or forced the rest of the states into the union. It was an important step toward dominance, yet it proved too shallow, as no real loyalty was achieved. Furthermore, even the economic gain from it remained largely limited.

A map of the German Confederation, with Prussia colored in blue (lighter blue are territories outside of the confederation). Source: https://commons.wikimedia.org

The federal security issue was essentially an attempt to create a unified Germanic army that would defend all the states. The Prussians tried to create such an organization both in 1818, when Napoleon's occupation was still an open sore, as well as in 1830, when France went through another revolution, deposing one branch of the Bourbons for another. In both instances, the foreign threat was seen as the lesser of two evils. The question of a joint military was reheated in 1840 when a new French government demanded reinstating France's borders on the Rhine. The issue was resolved peacefully, as neither side was really looking to start another war, but a more direct threat faced the German Confederation: its weakness. Its response was to create a string of federal fortresses, mostly toward France, as well as adding steps toward integration of the different Germanic armies. However, these never managed to lead to a proper fighting force, as bureaucracy and diplomacy made it quite inefficient and slow.

In the end, neither the Customs Union nor the Federal Army brought Prussia closer to dominating the Germanic lands. It was still necessary to maintain decent relations with Austria and to even cooperate with them at certain points, like, for example, agreeing to a military union in the case of a French attack during the 1840 Rhine Crisis. Nevertheless, such actions did bring Prussia some respect, especially as it almost always seemed more progressive and liberal than Austria. Yet, most states remained wary of Berlin's pretensions, at least the governments.

The common people's nationalistic ideas of a unified German people began to arise, mostly as a response to Napoleon's occupation and subsequent French nationalistic outbursts. Since Prussia bore the brunt of the fight against the French, it also gained slightly more attraction in such circles as well. This is especially evident in the 1813 campaign, which became known as the War of Liberation, indicating its "Pan-Germanic" character. However, during Frederick William III's reign, these outbursts of German nationalism were rare, as nationalism itself was only in its infancy, far from the political and ideological driving force it would become.

In internal affairs, Prussia was facing its own dualism. On the one hand, because of the supposedly "dangerous" fallout of the French Revolution, there was a growing conservative political wing. Its representatives worked hard, mostly against any kind of populist groups, as well as progressive politicians aiming at transforming Prussia into a parliamentary monarchy. These forces prevailed in the end, with many progressives losing their posts, Humboldt being one of them. The liberal dream of a national assembly was stifled for a while. Furthermore, conservatives reduced the local diets into more of an advisory body than proper political representation. The liberal vision was not achieved, at least partially thanks to the internal squabbles between liberals but also because Frederick William III sought to appease the Russians, who were still leaning heavily toward absolutism. The Prussian king even married off one of his daughters to the Russian tsar, allowing for these connections to be even tighter for a while.

Regardless of that, the progressive spirit remained. This was most notable in the education system, which remained among the best in the world, with some 80 percent of children attending. It continued to produce citizens who could at least read, but in many cases, they could do even more than that. That played in hand with the growing economy and industrialization that was picking up pace. Not only did it allow for more professional workers, but the state also opened institutes for technology, importing the knowledge and technology that were needed to kickstart the Prussian industrial revolution. Such modernization was eased by the fact that the Rhineland territories were already quite urban and were considerably rich in coal. The Ruhr region was notable for that kind of natural riches. Thus, the economy was also growing toward a progressive industrial future, but it should be noted it wasn't yet booming. Major improvements came in the late 1830s with the first railways, which connected Berlin and Potsdam. This new transportation technology would soon expand across the kingdom.

Another aspect of Frederick William III's later reign was achieving some kind of bureaucratic and national unity. After 1815, Prussia gained various new territories and had to incorporate new systems and nationalities into the state. These were achieved in various ways, but it proved especially difficult with the new Polish subjects in Posen. They were among the few non-Germanic nations within Prussia, and they were certainly the largest non-German-speaking minority. On top of that, they never came to terms with losing their homeland. To some extent, they and other minorities went through the Germanization process but never completely or too aggressively. Additionally, more urban western provinces were a stronghold of progressive civic ideas, somewhat counterbalancing the more conservative eastern lands.

Another disbalance could be found in the laws. While the state worked on once again equalizing the whole system, the results varied. Some new provinces completely adopted the Prussian system, some adopted parts of it, and some acknowledged it merely on paper. In that regard, probably the most notable difference was that the Edict of Emancipation remained active only in the "old" Prussian lands, making only parts of Prussia open to Jews. Apart from that, Frederick William III also tried to unify all the Protestant denominations in Prussia under the so-called Union of Evangelical Churches. It was meant to unify both the Lutherans and Calvinists without changing their religious practices and beliefs. Despite that, the religious unification didn't go too smoothly, as it included some coercive measures, as well as local schisms.

In the end, Frederick William III ended his reign peacefully in June 1840. His rule was marked by great turmoil, somewhat distorting our image of his capabilities, but he managed to keep Prussia afloat. Regardless of that, it was clear that, with his rule, the ideas of a strong and independent Hohenzollern monarch came to an end. He was the first king whose reign was heavily dependent on his ministers and whose power was no longer fully absolute. He was succeeded by his eldest son, who became known as King Frederick William IV. The new king was well educated in various fields, but he never showed any special talents, except in drawing. Since his childhood days, he seemed more of a daydreamer; thus, he grew into an avid romanticist. Additionally, Frederick William IV was a deeply religious and pious person. All of that combined to form a person in love with the romanticized image of medieval Germany, which dictated his policies throughout his reign.

That kind of idealized vision of politics and the monarchy make Frederick William IV hard to categorize. He dangled between the liberals and conservatives, leaning to one or another from issue to issue. On the one hand, he championed more liberal politics, such as reduced censorship and tolerance toward religious schismatics and the Poles. The new king also made local diets convene more regularly and rehabilitated some earlier reformers who had fallen into disfavor. Yet, in contrast, he refused to accept ideas of a constitution or national assembly and also retained some sense of a conservative stance toward social class issues.

However, this doesn't mean that Frederick William actually agreed with either side; rather, he wanted to create some sort of reconciliation between the two political forces in hopes of restoring the Prussian subjects' faith in the monarchy and rekindling some sort of medieval feudal loyalty. Some of his romanticized views came from his religiousness, as he saw the kingship as a divine right, giving him a holy insight into the needs of his subjects. Such politics went against liberal constitutional-parliamentary ideas, but they also didn't appeal to the conservative circles since it seemed he wanted to recreate the medieval state. To almost everyone in government, it seemed as if he was ignoring reality.

A photograph of Frederick William IV from 1847. Source: https://commons.wikimedia.org

Despite his political anachronism, Frederick William displayed impressive economic progressiveness. Since his youth, he had favored the idea of transforming Prussia from an agricultural to an industrial state, supporting the import of foreign technology and expertise. To aid in that kind of development, the king and the state supported infrastructural expansion, with the most notable being the railway system. Unlike his predecessor, Frederick William IV not only gave his wholehearted support for railway expansion, but it was also his preferred mode of transportation. Thus, during his reign, the Prussian textile industry, coal mining, and mechanical engineering picked up speed. These industries were concentrated in Ruhr and Silesia, which were traditional manufacturing centers, as well as around Berlin. Industrial and economic output slowly grew, adding an overall positive effect on the state's wealth. However, it simultaneously created a new set of social issues, as the new urban working class began showing signs of discontent with the political system, as well as their working and living conditions. Thus, Prussia was constantly plagued by minor worker revolts and strikes, with the most famous being the Silesian Weavers' Revolt of 1844, during which Frederick William IV was the target of a failed assassination attempt from a disgruntled former civil servant.

A painting of the developing industry near Berlin. Source: https://commons.wikimedia.org

The king's response to the issue was once again somewhat paradoxical. He personally donated money to associations of the working class. Yet, at the same time, he issued the General Prussian Industrial Code of 1845, which banned strikes, making them punishable by imprisonment. It seems that Frederick William felt compassion for his subjects, as he never tried to suppress their revolts too harshly, but he wanted to keep the "third class" from rising and disrupting the social balance. However, he failed to recognize that the balance had already been disrupted. During the 1840s, there was a noticeable process of pauperization of the lower classes, followed by occasional food shortages. These issues proved to be the most common motivators of protests, which notably remained local in nature. Some scholars tried to connect the issues with the Malthusian idea of population outgrowing the food supply, yet it wasn't true. Much like industry, agriculture was also developing due to new technologies, like artificial fertilizers, which significantly increased food production. Nevertheless, those advances didn't make agriculture resistant to natural and biological misfortunes, which caused short-term shortages. The more apparent reason should be found in the high number of people moving to the cities looking for jobs, which made unskilled labor quite cheap.

Apart from that, it should be noted that the noble class was also slowly losing ground. For decades, starting from the Napoleonic Wars, aristocrats were slowly losing their estates, a trend noticeable in Europe as a whole. By the 1850s, in certain areas of Prussia, they held only some 50 percent of their lands from the beginning of the 19th century. With that, the nobility was slowly losing its material influence in favor of the "new rich," the industrials and merchants. Nevertheless, the aristocracy kept a strong influence on politics, and the two upper classes often managed to find common interests. The final aspect of the changing social and political scene was the evolution toward so-called "popular politics." As the masses became more literate, newspapers and pamphlets fueled political debates. These were often illustrated with various caricatures, adding a visual aspect while making the message easier to understand. Songs and smaller theatrical pieces at carnivals were also popular media for political agitation and expression. Overall, it was the ongoing politicization of popular culture, making politics part of everyday life. More importantly, it also began reaching much wider corners of society, meaning it was no longer limited to the higher classes.

Amidst such changes, Frederick William IV wanted to expand the railway network to directly connect Brandenburg with the Rhine provinces. This was partially caused by economic necessity but even more by the need for military transport and a stronger political connection. However, such an investment required sizable funds, prompting the government to search for a loan. The only problem was that a law from Hardenberg's time prevented the state from raising credit without the approval of a national assembly. It was, in essence, a combination of all the provincial diets into a single body, and it was tasked only with approving the state loan. On the surface, it seemed like a law to prevent the state from spiraling into debt, but it was, in fact, left as a future tool to put pressure on the king to engage in liberal reforms. Despite that, Frederick William downplayed the possible complication and convened the United Diet in April 1847. It immediately became a controversial issue, as liberals saw it as a possible political platform. Nevertheless, the king warned them in the opening speech that there was no earthly power that could force him to sever his divine monarchical ties with his subjects for a sheet of paper, a metaphor for a constitution.

Unfortunately for him and his conservative supporters, the warning went unheard. Liberals of all kinds came together and acted in unison, blocking the loan. They demanded that the United Diet be transformed into a proper legislative body. In contrast, their conservative opponents were unable to work cohesively since their politics championed provincial autonomy, leaving them merely on a defensive footing. In June, the diet was adjourned without approving the loan. It was an anticlimactic end, but it signaled that social unrest was growing and that the Prussian people wanted to finally put an end to the absolute monarchy by creating a constitution and a parliament. It was a powder keg waiting to explode. The government felt that pressure, especially the king, who became a primary target of caricatures and political attacks. In response, censorship was somewhat tightened, as well as police control and scrutiny. The state reverted to engaging in political and social oppression.

The social storm was brewing, but it wasn't limited only to Prussia or the Germanic states. People across Europe were beginning to voice their displeasure with the dominant conservatism, demanding more liberal and democratic politics.

Uprisings, revolts, and revolutions began spreading across the continent, starting with Switzerland in late 1847 and the Italian states in early 1848. However, proper revolutionary zeal began to catch on only after the February 1848 Revolution in France. It was fueled by nationalist and republican ideals, which quickly caught on in the already socially unstable Prussia, as well as other states of the German Confederation. The first major protest in Berlin began in early March. Clashes between demonstrators and police ensued, leaving some casualties. The court was unsure how to proceed. Some hawkish elements, including the king's younger brother, Prince Wilhelm (William), wanted the military to stifle the revolt. Others were in favor of a milder stance or even a compromise. It was only after the fall of the conservative government in Vienna that Frederick William decided to buckle and avoid further confrontations. Instead of fighting the revolution, he would lead it.

Rioting in the streets of Berlin in 1848. Source: https://commons.wikimedia.org

On March 18th, the public gathered in front of Frederick William's palace, where he tried to publicly proclaim the convening of the United Diet and the drafting of the constitution. However, the presence of armed troops caused panic amongst the protesters, and due to this confusion, a massive clash between the protesters and guards ensued. Once again, Frederick William decided to de-escalate the situation. Instead of unleashing the army on the protesters, he withdrew it from the city while staying himself. This appalled many, as it was seen as the subjects infringing upon the monarch's rights. It even prompted the short exile of Prince Wilhelm, who expressed his utmost displeasure with the act. Nevertheless, the king stood his ground and allowed the formation of a national assembly tasked with drafting the constitution. However, once given the power, protestors fractured. There were various liberal and democratic ideals at play, but most importantly, there was a strong radical wing that was leaning toward what we could say Marxist ideas. Their presence pushed many toward the liberal center, lessening the assembly's revolutionary spirit.

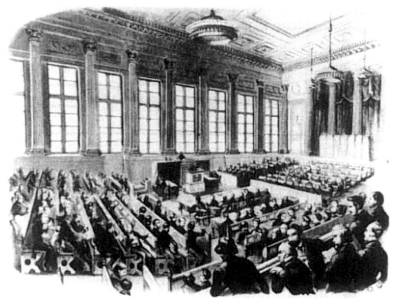

A wood engraving of a session of the United Diet. Source: https://commons.wikimedia.org

All the while, Frederick William negotiated with the representatives about the constitution, but it was hard to find common ground. Then, in late November, unsatisfied with the overall development of the changes, the assembly called for a tax strike. For the king, it was a step too far, so he enacted martial law and dispersed the protestors. By then, revolutionary zeal was largely gone, and it proved to be an easy and quick victory for the government. The United Diet was officially dissolved on December 5th, but Frederick William followed that by issuing his own constitution that was an agreeable middle ground to gather support from most of the liberals and moderate conservatives. Additionally, such a political approach alienated the more radical elements on both sides of the political spectrum, which allowed Frederick William to begin his work on restoring Prussia's social unity.

However, democratic and liberal ideas were only one aspect of the European Revolutions of 1848. The other major aspect was nationalism. In the Germanic states, it posed a question of the unification of the German people into a single state. The main proponent of such ideas was the Frankfurt National Assembly, the first elected parliament of the German Confederation. Ultimately, its main goal was to formulate how and on what basis Germany should reunite into a single state. The assembly began its work in May 1848, with the main issue being if Austria should be accepted into the new state and in what scope. There was also the question of if the state should have a king and if the post should be elective or hereditary. Ideas of a republic were also brought in. While the other Germanic states were still struggling with their own internal revolutions, Frederick William IV had already accepted, though cautiously, the idea of unification. He said that Prussia would become a part of Germany, all the while carrying an armband of the German national colors: red, black, and gold (or yellow). In essence, the idea of restoring the German Empire was in accordance with his romantic interpretation of history, but the Prussian king seemed reluctant that it was the "proper" way to do it.

A drawing of Frederick William IV riding through Berlin after supporting the goal of German unity. Source: https://commons.wikimedia.org

Even before the Frankfurt National Assembly convened, Prussia and Frederick William accepted the role as the protectors of the German realm. In early 1848, they clashed with the Kingdom of Denmark over the future of the Schleswig and Holstein provinces. Those territories were ruled under a personal union of the Danish king while still being part of the German Confederation as separate entities. Pressured by inheritance issues and a wave of nationalism, the Danish king tried to annex and integrate the two provinces into Denmark. That move outraged the local German population, as well as the rest of the confederation. In response, Prussia sent a part of its army to Schleswig and Holstein in April of that year. It had the German Confederation's official endorsement, and the Prussians quickly pushed the Danish defenders back to Jutland. The other major powers were quick to react to this move, though. Most notably, Britain and Russia warned Frederick William he was going too far, asking for a withdrawal and a peaceful mediation.

This left Prussia in a tight spot, strung between the Frankfurt National Assembly and the threat of a much greater confrontation. In the end, Frederick William buckled and signed a treaty with Denmark in August 1848. However, part of the German Federal Army, which had gathered by then, continued the struggle, claiming they were under the jurisdiction of the assembly, not the Prussian king. The separate peace was seen as Frederick William's betrayal of German nationalism since he had acted on his own accord.

Nevertheless, the Frankfurt National Assembly was still grateful for the assistance of Prussian troops in suppressing violent radical revolts in Baden. Overall, though not successfully, Prussia acted as a guardian of the German Confederation. Thus, when the Frankfurt National Assembly finally reached its conclusion, it decided to create a nation-state without Austria, as it had too much of a non-German population. By March 1849, it sent an official offer of the imperial crown to Frederick William. Surprisingly, he rejected the offer. It was not that he didn't dream of being a German emperor, but rather, it was because the way the assembly attempted to do it was wrong in his eyes. First, he wanted Austria to be kept a part of it. Secondly, he felt that a national diet didn't have the right to offer him anything; only the institution of the old medieval elector princes could. Frederick William replied that the assembly could ask him to be an emperor but that it didn't have the right to offer him a crown.

That rejection brought the Frankfurt National Assembly to an end. It was a clear defeat of the nationalistic ideas of unification, at least for a while. Yet, at the same time, it showcased that Prussia had become the most influential Germanic state. For the first time in history, it overshadowed Austria.

Chapter 9 – Final Evolution into the German Empire

Refusing the imperial crown from the national assembly may have ended revolutionary ideas for the unification of the German realm, but it wasn't the last attempt. Despite what might have seemed a defeat of nationalism, the desire for a united Germany remained strong.

The next attempt at fulfilling the German dream came from Frederick William IV. After refusing to be crowned emperor, he began working to form the so-called Erfurt Union. This was a federation with other Germanic states, excluding Austria, based on arrangements with their rulers. The other monarchs expressed some initial interest in this, laying ground to its formal existence in mid-1849. However, it never received much public support, and hammering exact agreements among more than twenty sovereign rulers proved to be an impossible task. Another issue was Austria's stance. Initially, Vienna showed signs of interest, as it was proposed that the Erfurt Union would, in turn, be loosely tied with Austria in a broader coalition or confederacy. Yet, by late 1849, the Habsburgs turned aggressively against it, seemingly when the other Germanic states began showing their doubts, with some even leaving the federation. Instead, they began advocating the resurrection of the, by then, defunct German Confederation.

By early 1850, Berlin and Vienna were staring at a possible conflict. While Prussia continued with its attempts to realize the Erfurt Union, Austria partook in the revival of the old confederation. The final straw came in autumn when the ruler of Hesse-Kassel asked for the German Confederation's military aid. Since that land was straddled between Prussian territory, it led to further friction, alarming Frederick William enough to order full mobilization. However, Austria was backed by the Russian Empire, making an open war impossible to win, which forced Prussia to back down. In late November 1850, the two Germanic states signed the so-called Punctation of Olmütz, forcing Prussia back into the confederation with a promise of some reforms. Another point that was also added was that the Schleswig-Holstein issue would be dealt with by the German Confederation as a whole, as the First Schleswig War was still ongoing, though without direct Prussian interference. The end result of the Olmütz treaty was yet another diplomatic humiliation for Prussia, as it restored the German Confederations in 1851 with almost no changes, and there was also the final conclusion of peace with Denmark in 1852 under the tutelage of all major European powers. Schleswig and Holstein remained under Danish rule but with some constitutional limitations.

For many in Prussia, the Punctation of Olmütz was another humiliation, showing that most major powers still looked down on it. Yet, Frederick William had more pressing matters to deal with. Though the revolution was stopped, there were still some smoldering remnants, especially in the Rhineland region. Most of the protests were led by the more radical leftists, who were influenced by Karl Marx, and the king knew their ideas had to be suppressed. Apart from that, the state needed to be reformed to follow the new constitution. Putting down rebellions in the western provinces proved relatively easy, as the radicals never had wide support. Reforming the state proved a bit more difficult since the system needed some fine-tuning. The Landtag of Prussia (*Preußischer Landtag*, the Prussian parliament) was formed, and it was divided into two chambers. The upper consisted solely of the nobility, similar to the British House of Lords. Initially, its representatives were supposed to be at least partially elected, but by 1853, members were only appointed by the king. The lower house was the House of Representatives, whose members were elected.

However, the voting was based on the three-class suffrage system. That meant the voters were divided into three voting classes based on their income, with all electing an equal number of representatives. This meant that the wealthiest 4.7 percent of the population had the same voting power as the 12.7 percent of the second class and the 82.6 percent of the third class. Thus, the new system favored the rich and nobles. Additionally, under the new constitution, ministers answered only to the king, who kept all his executive powers and retained the power of the judicial veto. The monarch also retained supreme command of the army and the right to sign treaties and declare wars. Finally, the sovereign wielded the right to amend the constitution, which Frederick William IV did several times up until 1857. Apart from the central government, local governments and the legal framework were tuned for the new system, once again aiming at the equalization and functionality of the state. The final change was the addition of new taxes, although old taxes were also reformed. This increased the state's revenue, which, in turn, allowed the government to increase its investments and speed up the development of the economy, most notably industry.

All the while, Prussia remained largely inactive and neutral in diplomatic matters. Thus, when the other European powers went to war against Russia in the Crimean War (1854–1856), it remained on the sidelines. However, it marked the break between the Russo-Austrian alliance, which would prove to be vital for Prussia.

Similarly, Berlin remained neutral when the Italian War of 1859 erupted. This was a conflict between the Habsburgs and the Kingdom of Sardinia, which was backed by France and sought Italian unification. The Prussian Army was mobilized to secure its western frontiers, but its alliance negotiations with Vienna failed. In the end, the Italo-French alliance won, creating fertile ground for the proclamation of the Kingdom of Italy in 1861.

The war showcased several important international factors. First, nationalistic ideals were still strong, and the unification of Italy reheated the question of a German nation-state. Secondly, it exhibited the loss of Austrian power while, at the same time, boosting the reputation of the new French Empire. The latter had become an imperial monarchy in 1852 after a coup, and it was ruled by Emperor Napoleon III, Napoleon's nephew. Finally, it emphasized the relative weakness of Prussia through its inactivity, prompting some observers to question its status as a major power.

This irked Prince Wilhelm, who became regent in place of his brother in 1857. Frederick William IV had suffered a series of strokes, rendering him almost speechless and mentally impaired. Since he had no children, he willingly gave power to his younger brother. At the time, Wilhelm was sixty years old, and he was militarily oriented and a former staunch conservative who quickly adapted to the new system. Thus, from his perspective, the only way to acquire recognition and political influence was through a strong army. He began leaning toward such developments at the start of the regency, but he really picked up the pace after his brother's death in 1861. Once he became King Wilhelm I, he immediately pushed for the renewal of military strength, which had not been significantly improved since 1806; in fact, it had somewhat deteriorated. The liberal-led assembly tried to block Wilhelm by refusing to fund it, which prompted him to install Otto von Bismarck as his prime minister. Bismarck, who was a crafty politician, managed to outplay the liberals. Together with Minister of War Albrecht von Roon and Chief of Staff Helmuth von Moltke, a famous field marshal, they began reforming the army.

An 1857 photo of Wilhelm I (top) and an 1860s illustration of Bismarck, Roon, and Moltke in said order (bottom).
Source: https://commons.wikimedia.org

Moltke's idea was to increase the number of active soldiers, adopt new types of arms, master quicker and better mobilization, improve communication and deployment using modern technologies, and create a more professional and well-trained officer corps. While the field marshal worked on these, Bismarck worked on securing his political position and began forging the path to the ultimate goal of his government: the unification of Germany. The first real test came in 1863 when the Schleswig-Holstein situation flared up once again. A new Danish king had tried to merge Schleswig with Denmark, breaching the 1852 treaty. Of course, the German Confederation immediately reacted. In late 1863, a small Federal contingent entered Holstein before Austria and Prussia jointly declared war against Denmark in January of the following year. It was a relatively short war, lasting only a few months. A German victory was almost certain from the beginning since the Danes received no international backing due to their breach of an international treaty. It ended in August of 1864, with both provinces officially ceded to the German Confederation under the direct and shared control of Austria and Prussia.

The war and victory showcased two important things. One was that the Prussian military reforms were moving in the right direction. Its achievements were really spectacular, especially in comparison with the Austrians. The second thing the war illustrated was that military leadership functioned better when it was under the primacy of political leadership. Bismarck was the conductor of all activities, even though his stance angered some of the generals. All the while, elderly Wilhelm I was slowly relinquishing the reins of the state to the prime minister, though not without his influence. What ensued was often depicted as Bismarck's grand scheme of some sort, yet in reality, he just proved to be an adaptive and cunning politician. The situation at Schleswig and Holstein remained unresolved, to a degree on porpoise, creating increasing tensions between Austria and Prussia.

While the hostilities were slowly heating up, Bismarck went on to create fertile diplomatic ground for a confrontation with the Habsburgs. First, he secured an alliance with the Kingdom of Italy since parts of Italy were still under Austrian control. Then, he secured Russian neutrality, which was easily achieved, for Saint Petersburg was still hostile toward Vienna. Britain was already uninterested in German affairs, which means the final nail in the coffin was France. Bismarck ensured Paris wouldn't intervene, giving a vague unwritten promise to Napoleon III that he could expand in Belgium and Luxemburg in return.

By the summer of 1866, Austria and Prussia were on the brink of war. Both sides began a series of local and partial mobilizations. Austria tried to unanimously convene the local Holstein diet, which gave Bismarck an excuse to send troops to occupy it on the basis of Austria's infringement of the joint sovereignty. In response, Vienna turned to the Federal Assembly. Most members of the German Confederation condemned the invasion and voted in favor of their mobilization against Prussia. The Prussian representative eventually walked out on the assembly, stating that, for Berlin, the German Confederation was dissolved. The war began on June 14th, with Italy joining five days later. On the Prussian side stood a number of smaller Germanic states, with most of the large ones, like Bavaria, Saxony, and Hanover, siding with Austria. At the start of the war, most observers expected an Austrian victory, as they still considered the Prussian forces to be the underdog. However, Moltke and his reforms were quick to prove them wrong.

While the majority of Prussian forces began their offensive in Bohemia (the modern-day Czech Republic), its secondary troops dealt with the Hanoverian troops, as they were an immediate threat to Prussia's rear. Then, according to Moltke's grand plan, the main Prussian Army in Bohemia sought a quick and decisive battle. Somewhat unwillingly, the Austrians met the invading forces at the Battle of Königgrätz (present-day Sadová) on July 3rd, 1866. There, despite their ineffective artillery, Prussia's superior training, officer leadership, and innovative infantry rifles won the day against the Austrians. Although the Prussians were marginally outnumbered, they managed to inflict around twenty-two thousand casualties and as many captured on the Austrian army. While the main force continued to advance through the Czech Republic and Slovakia, other Prussian troops defeated the Saxon and Bavarian troops. The Austrians, knowing they were facing total defeat, asked for peace on July 22nd, ending the war in a mere seven weeks.

A painting of the Battle of Königgrätz.
Source: https://commons.wikimedia.org

Bismarck was keen on accepting the peace without prolonging the war. He was concerned major powers might choose to intervene, and the economic factor was also a concern. Furthermore, the prime minister wanted to avoid too much revanchism from Austria or other Germanic states. The peace was ratified in Prague in late August, but not without French interference. Prussia annexed Schleswig, Holstein, Hanover, Hesse-Kassel, Nassau, and Frankfurt, while the rest of the northern Germanic states were organized into the North German Confederation. Prussia basically controlled the confederation's military and foreign relations; in other words, these states were basically just a step away from annexation.

The ultimate result of the war was Austria's exclusion from German affairs, most notably the question of unification. The only way forward from there was a union without Austria or any other Habsburgian lands—a union referred to as Lesser Germany (*Kleindeutschland*). The victory of 1866 also cemented Bismarck's government, though he still faced staunch opposition, and nationalistic fervor began boiling over. It was only a matter of time before Prussia made the final step toward a German nation-state.

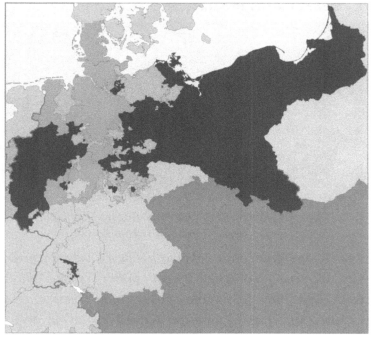

Map of the Austro-Prussian War of 1866—Austrian Empire (red), Austrian allies (pink), Prussian allies (light blue), Prussia (dark blue), Prussia acquisitions (cyan), and neutral states (green). Source: https://commons.wikimedia.org

Initially, Bismarck thought it might be possible to achieve a peaceful unification, but the southern Germanic states remained quite suspicious of Prussia. He tried to alleviate this problem in 1868 by forming an all-German Customs Parliament (*Zollparlament*), which would strengthen Prussian ties with the southern Germanic states. However, the attempt was ultimately a failure. By then, Bismarck realized that what Prussia needed was an external enemy that would bring the entire German nation together. France fit this role perfectly. Emperor Napoleon III had remained unsatisfied after the Austro-Prussian War. Instead of leaving the German realm fractured and weakened as Napoleon had hoped, France stared at an enlarged and strengthened Prussia. In 1867, Napoleon tried to buy Luxembourg, but Bismarck pulled diplomatic strings to prevent that from happening. This went against their spoken agreement, and it stirred up resentment against Franco-Prussian relations.

Once again, many historians frame the upcoming series of events, starting with the Luxembourg crisis, as part of Bismarck's "grand design." However, once again, he merely proved his political skills and flexibility to utilize opportunities the best he could. Even the Customs Parliament played a double role; apart from trying to sway the southern states, it was also aimed at irking the French, as it was another step toward unification. From Napoleon's perspective, a united Germany was the last thing France could afford since it posed all kinds of threats, not to mention thwarting his plans. Bismarck was aware of that when he continued to build on the tensions between Paris and Berlin, all the while handling internal political struggles with both the liberals and more radical conservatives. In the background, Moltke was finalizing his reforms, introducing a new artillery piece to resolve the issues from the Austro-Prussian War while also leaning into better training, expanding the army, and utilizing new technologies, like railways and the telegraph.

Continuing to masterfully play both German and French nationalistic feelings and constantly pouring oil onto the fire, Bismarck used every opportunity to provoke Napoleon into declaring war. For his plans to work, Prussia had to be in a defensive position. Among many smaller incitements, a particularly fertile one started in late 1869 when the Spanish Parliament offered a crown to Wilhelm's cousin. Initially, every member of the Hohenzollern family was against it, but Bismarck plotted for the cousin to accept. While he was working on that, he caused a few smaller provocations, but to no avail. Then, in the spring of 1870, he finally persuaded Wilhelm's cousin to accept the throne, causing an immediate reaction in Paris. It seemed all was going according to plan, but then Wilhelm I intervened and put a stop to the Spanish affair. Bismarck was crushed, and he almost gave up before the French made a crucial mistake. Their ambassador tried to gain further promises and public statements from the Prussian king. It was too much for Wilhelm, who simply refused. He sent notice to Bismarck about the conversation, which the prime minister used to create a modified version in which the talk seemed more abrupt and impolite, a move that aimed to stir the fiery nationalists on both sides. The message, the so-called Ems Dispatch, was circulated across European newspapers, including in France.

For Paris, this insult was the cherry on top, and they declared war on July 19th, 1870. Bismarck's plan had finally worked. The southern Germanic states immediately joined Prussia, both because of their existing agreements but also because of nationalistic fervor. The idea of yet another Napoleon ravaging the German realm was unacceptable for most. The rest of Europe was decidedly neutral in the conflict. On the one hand, Napoleon didn't have any more allies nor sympathies, while Bismarck was already on friendly terms with Russia and Italy. Austria was still recovering, and Britain seemed to be at terms with Prussian-led Germany. Nevertheless, all the observers expected a longer war and slightly favored the French, as its military was still considered to be among the best in the world. However, from the onset, it was clear that the Prussian military reforms were paying off. They mobilized the army faster and produced more soldiers, even though Prussia had fewer citizens. Then came the first serious clashes in early August, most notably Spicheren and Froeschwiller Woerth, which all ended in Prussian victories.

A 1910 painting depicting the Prussian infantry during the Franco-Prussian War. Source: https://commons.wikimedia.org

The Prussian Army advanced through France in three columns, taking a series of victories against the passive French defenders. By mid-August, the main French fighting force was besieged in Metz, which consisted of their best troops. Napoleon III gathered what remained of the French military and attempted to relieve Metz, but he was forced away from it, so he headed to the fortress of Sedan. Once there, he was forced into a battle against the numerically superior Prussian Army and its allies. Napoleon was defeated and captured, along with the entire army. Soon afterward, Metz surrendered as well, and the rest of the Prussian forces moved to besiege Paris. The French imperial regime crumbled, giving way to yet another republic.

Despite that, France was determined to fight. The people's nationalism was too strong. The new government in Paris tried to relieve some pressure by organizing new armies, but those ad hoc regiments were no match against the well-trained Prussians. Thus, on January 26th, an armistice was signed, officially ending the hostilities on January 28th, 1871. The entire war lasted roughly six months and proved to be nothing more than a pure demonstration of Prussian power. France seemed like a third-rate state compared to it, something that completely shocked Europe.

To put it in perspective, the combined Prusso-German forces had some 140,000 casualties and captured soldiers. The entire French Army had 140,000 dead and as many wounded, while an additional 750,000 were captured. Such a conclusive victory finally proved the worth of Moltke's reforms, as the basis of the Prussian victory lay in enlarging the army through universal conscription, ensuring better-trained soldiers and officer cadre, and using new communication and transportation technologies. And all of this was topped off with aggressive strategies and mission-based tactics, allowing for a more flexible army. However, the military remained under the government's reins, something of which Bismarck continuously reminded the military leaders, which caused some friction.

While the war was still ongoing, Bismarck began negotiating with the southern Germanic states about joining the new confederation. When they accepted, the Prussian prime minister proposed going a step further and restoring the German Empire. Thanks to his political machinations, which included bribery, he managed to gather enough votes in the Federal Assembly to proclaim the formation of the German Empire (*Deutsches Kaiserreich*) on January 18th, 1871, in Versailles. It was a political double entendre, as it humiliated France and marked the anniversary of the Hohenzollerns' formal inauguration as the kings in Prussia, which happened in 1701.

A later rendition of the proclamation of the German Empire at Versailles.
Source: https://commons.wikimedia.org

The unification was thus finalized. The Prussian king now became German Emperor Wilhelm I while still holding onto his title of king. This was only further formalized when the French were forced to recognize the empire in their peace treaty, with Bismarck going on to further humiliate them. He annexed Alsace and Lorraine, border territories near Germany, which were also industrial centers of France. Additionally, he forced a huge indemnity on the losers. It was, in a way, payback for what Napoleon had done to Prussia and the rest of Germany, especially when considering that the German occupation of northern France wasn't handled lightly. Thus, Prussia, now transformed into the German Empire, managed to fulfill its long-lasting dream of uniting the German people and cementing its position as a major world power. An additional bonus was that its lightning-fast victories also created a myth of German military superiority, which often stretched back to the time of Frederick the Great. At least for a while, Prussia's and Germany's future seemed bright.

Epilogue

The newly formed German Empire used the constitution of the North German Confederation as its basis. Thus, formally speaking, it was a tighter federal union of twenty-six entities, one of them being the Kingdom of Prussia. With that in mind, it could be said that Prussia "survived" the unification, as did the other Germanic states. However, from 1871 onward, its history became more of a part of German history than an individual story. Regardless, it should be noted that due to its central role in German unification, as well as the fact that the Hohenzollern dynasty ruled the empire, Germany was very much based on Prussian culture, traditions, and politics. Other states were slowly remodeled to fit the Prussian state system. This wasn't a significant change in most cases, as many Germanic states were already following the successful Prussian system, and their economies had also been interlinked for decades.

Over the next roughly forty years, the German Empire continued to grow and develop as a state. Most notable was the industrial boom, which placed it in the top three world economies. Politically speaking, it continued to swing between the conservatives and liberals, and the Prussian cultural model remained the most prominent. Emperor Wilhelm I continued his reign until 1888, and he was succeeded by his son, Frederick III, who ruled for a short time before his own son took over. Under Emperor Wilhelm II, Bismarck finally lost his place as the imperial chancellor in 1890. With that, the once-content German Empire set its sights on bigger goals, joining the colonial race while also trying to expand its influence. The combination of nationalistic and power politics pushed it toward a confrontation with the other major powers. The long-lasting tensions finally erupted with World War I in 1914, when Germany and Austria fought against Russia, Britain, and France. In 1918, Germany was defeated, with the empire being dissolved. The Hohenzollerns were forced to abdicate.

Nevertheless, Prussia as an entity survived as a "free state" or one of the constituent republics of the German Weimar Republic. The new government considered breaking up Prussia into smaller states, as it comprised roughly 60 percent of German territories, but conservative elements preserved it in its entirety. During the 1920s and even more so during the 1930s, a new wave of modern nationalism swept Europe and Germany, leading to the rise of the Nazi Party and Adolf Hitler. The new regime had a love-hate relationship with Prussia. On the one hand, they glorified its past, most notably Frederick II and its role in Germany's unification, and also adopted its militaristic and cultural heritage. On the other hand, they weren't fond of some of its traditional and conservative ideas. Thus, by the start of World War II, Nazi propaganda highjacked Prussian history and mythos, warping it to fit their perspective of the world. Their propaganda was so powerful that when the Third Reich was defeated, the Allies saw the Nazis as merely the latest example of "militant Prussianism." This finally led to the end of Prussia. Its territories were divided up, with large chunks remaining outside of German borders, while the rest was renamed to fit their pre-Prussian names. Thus, the region around Berlin became known as Brandenburg once again, bringing the tale of Prussia full circle.

Conclusion

The history of Prussia is a tale of ups and downs, destruction and revival, a tale of constant change and reforms in pursuit of survival and power. It showed a small and inconsequential Germanic state beating all odds and traversing the dangerous and destructive labyrinth of history to become one of the mightiest nations in the world. At some points, its fate dwindled on the edge, depending solely on the stubbornness of its leaders. At other times, it managed to take great strides forward, fueled by the genius and foresight of its rulers. In that aspect, its history depicts all the greatness that can be achieved through hard work and a bit of luck. Nevertheless, it is also a reminder that no nation is too big to fail and that no idea is too pure to be tainted. A great power that needed roughly three centuries to rise to its full power was toppled in mere decades, taking its ideals with it. As such, it is also a cautionary tale, reminding us that staying humble when achieving greatness is a virtue. Finally, it is a story of the interconnectedness of hubris and humility that entwines human lives.

Hopefully, this short guide gave you a basic idea of how Prussian history developed over the centuries, showing you that simplifications of it being just "good" or "bad" isn't how we should judge countries, nations, and people. History, as well as present life, is rarely that simple. It is a thought that is always worth remembering when judging both individuals and groups. Another important moral of Prussia's story is that constant change and adaptiveness make a difference, as one should recognize one's chances and take them. In the end, all of these lessons are what makes history worth reading and understanding. It teaches us about our present and our lives and helps us understand each other and the larger picture in which we live.

Part 2: The Franco-Prussian War

A Captivating Guide to the War of 1870 between the French Empire and German States and the Role Otto von Bismarck Played in the Unification of Germany

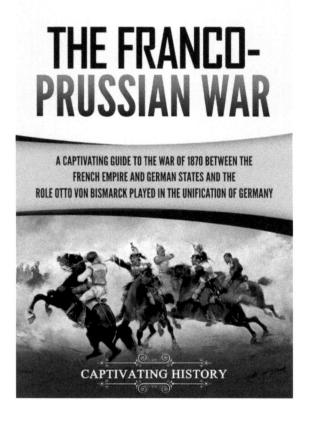

Introduction

When talking about 19th-century European history, the spotlight is often directed at Napoleon Bonaparte and his wars in the early 1800s. The rest of the century is somehow lumped together, peppered with stories of industrial developments and social and cultural evolutions. It was almost as if this period of time was a breather before the Great War of 1914. Such an approach has its merits, as indeed the 19th century was largely shaped by the changes in technology due to the Industrial Revolution and by new ways of thinking, which were brought about by the French Revolution and Napoleon. However, an important note in European history that deserves to be noticed and talked about is the Franco-Prussian War of 1870.

The war itself was short, lasting barely six months. Despite that, it managed to shake the foundations of Europe. It showcased French weakness and the rising industrialization and modernization of Prussia. In a way, this conflict threw a wrench in the perceived balance of power after Napoleon's defeat. Not only that, but it led to the creation of the unified German Empire under the iron fist of Chancellor Bismarck. As such, unified Germany immediately became a political, economic, and military powerhouse in continental Europe, lagging only behind the British Empire. On the other hand, it led to the fall of the last monarchical regime in France. Furthermore, it showcased the importance of utilizing modernizations in technology and bureaucracy within the army, as the Prussian military model became a forerunner of the changes that were to come.

Yet, the outcomes and effects of the war, on their own, could still be deemed somewhat less significant, especially if one is not interested in military history. However, when combined together, it could be seen as the first major step toward the "war to end all wars," both in the form of the great game of national politics but also in transformations on the battlefield. As such, the Franco-Prussian War rippled across history, rightfully calling out for our attention in our quest to better understand our shared past.

Chapter 1 – A Long Road to War: A Short History of Franco-German Relations

Usually, the story of the Franco-Prussian War would begin in the decade prior to it, most notably due to Bismarck's ascendance to the position of Prussian chancellor. However, while such an introduction suffices for understanding the immediate causes of the war, to fully grasp the larger historical framework, it would be better to begin in the Middle Ages.

Most people know that in the early 9th century, Charlemagne the Great extended the Frankish Empire to cover modern-day France, Germany, the Low Countries, Switzerland, parts of northern Italy, and Austria, as well as parts of the Balkans, Hungary, the Czech Republic, and Spain. The pope crowned him as the Holy Roman emperor in 800. However, after Charlemagne's death, his heirs were unable to agree upon the succession to the throne. By the mid-9th century, the former empire had been split into three sections after a civil war among his grandsons. After the Treaty of Verdun in 843, Charlemagne's grandsons formed West Francia (the core of future France), East Francia (the core of future Germany), and

Middle Francia (situated between them, including the Low Countries and parts of northern Italy) under a provisional unity. Such a fragile state quickly dissolved. Middle Francia was the most brittle, as it lacked any sort of geographical or demographic unity, and by the end of the century, it had fractured. Meanwhile, East and West Francia began competing for parts of its territories, most notably the provinces today known as Alsace and Lorraine.

Map of the Frankish Empire division into what was to become Germany and France. Source: https://commons.wikimedia.org

Over the course of the next couple of centuries, two remaining Frankish states evolved into the more recognizable forms of France and Germany. In East Francia, that transformation came somewhat sooner, as, by the early 10th century, there was a growing idea that the kingdom belonged to the Germanic people, as it consisted of several Germanic tribes and peoples, like, for example, Frisians, Thuringii, and Saxons. Without delving too much into the formation of national identity, by the early 11th century, the official title of King of the Germans was in place. However, even prior to that, Otto I, a Germanic king of East Francia who was not a descendant of Charlemagne, managed to revive the Holy Roman Empire in 962. Thus, German history became more closely linked with the imperial legacy, especially as by the late 15th century, it became known as the Holy Roman Empire of the German Nations. Regardless of the name, it is vital to mention that the Holy Roman Empire after 962 was an elective monarchy, where several princes and dukes elected their sovereign after the passing of the ruler. Therefore, this empire was also a confederacy of sorts, as it legally recognized the constituent states had a degree of independence beneath the imperial crown.

In contrast, West Francia's transformation into France was more direct and easily understandable. For several centuries, its rulers held the title King of the Franks, indicating they were the rulers of said people. However, by the early 12th century, a new trend among the rulers was to present themselves as sovereigns of lands, not people. Thus, East Francia's rulers started to adopt the title King of France, indicating they ruled the Frankish territories. Over the years, the Franks became the French, while their nation became France. Such phrasing was solidified by the early 13th century. Another contrast between France and Germany is that the former remained a kingdom, though many have questioned the idea of how Germany was exactly the Holy Roman Empire. Yet, throughout the medieval period, the French kingdom was quite decentralized, as local lords had a lot of freedom in respect to their sovereign. Thus, like in the German Empire in the east, the strength of a king's rule depended on his own competence.

In a rather simplified story of these two nations, their trajectories were rather different. Beginning in the 12th century, the French kings began to reaffirm their rule over the country, slowly centralizing their power. With many ups and downs, they slowly transformed their kingdom from a feudal monarchy to an absolute monarchy by the 16th century. With that also came a more unified national feeling, as the French gradually began identifying more with their country than with their local identities. In contrast, the Holy Roman Empire, as a nation, weakened. Local dukes, kings, and princes grew in strength. In turn, though the population of the Germanic constituent states saw their common ancestry, their identities weren't as closely knit as among the French. Despite that, the Holy Roman Empire remained an important political factor. From the mid-15th century onward, it was almost continuously ruled by the Habsburg dynasty, despite the official electoral system still being in place.

With that, the Holy Roman Empire became part of a much larger conglomerate that is today sometimes referred to as the Habsburg monarchy. At its greatest extent, in the early 16th century, this Habsburgian political entity, in addition to the Holy Roman Empire, covered modern-day Austria, Hungary, parts of Poland, the Czech Republic, Slovakia, Slovenia, Croatia, Spain, Portugal, and their colonial empires across the globe. As such, the Habsburg monarchy, and with it, the Holy Roman Empire, became one of the main competitors of France. This relationship is comparable to the better-known Anglo-French relations. However, while the Habsburg Empire remained strong, Germany proper continued to wane. The Habsburgs centered their rule in Austria, while the rest of the Holy Roman Empire continued to fracture into smaller and weaker duchies and provinces. Their former glory was finally trampled when Germany became Europe's battlefield during the Thirty Years' War (1618–1648). By then, the Holy Roman Empire as a country was factually almost nonexistent, a mere shell of its former glory. Regardless, its title was still a source of prestige for the Habsburgs.

The 17th century saw the Kingdom of France at one of its highest points, most notably during the reign of the famous Louis XIV (r. 1643–1715), while Germany was a unified entity solely on paper. Nonetheless, the two collided on several occasions, as the Habsburgs waged war with the French over their influence of continental Europe, for example, the Nine Years' War (1688–1697) or the War of the Spanish Succession (1701–1714). Overall, France aimed at expanding its power and domain in Europe. As such, it saw a weak Germany as a favorable eastern neighbor, as it meant a less immediate threat from the Habsburgs and less opposition in general. Furthermore, it also meant a possible route for eastward expansion, as exhibited with frequent struggles to gain control over the Alsace and Lorraine provinces. As a result of numerous wars throughout the 17th and 18th centuries, these two regions were often swapped between the French and the Habsburgs.

After the death of Louis XIV, France began its downward trajectory, as his heirs proved somewhat less competent and lost some costly wars. Most notable was the Seven Years' War (1756–1763), which France waged primarily against the British. However, the start of this war proved to be a turning point in Franco-German relations. During this conflict, France actually allied with the Habsburgs, while Prussia, a rising Germanic state in the east, sided with the British. The origins of Prussia can be traced to the Teutonic knights establishing their domain centered around Königsberg (modern-day Kaliningrad) on the shores of the Baltic Sea. For most of its history, it was just one of many duchies in the region, subjugated either to the Holy Roman Empire or the Kingdom of Poland. Its rise to power came during the 17th century, with the first step coming in 1619 when it passed into the hands of the Hohenzollern dynasty.

This was important because the Hohenzollerns held other estates in Germany, most notably Brandenburg and its capital of Berlin, while Prussia was officially a Polish fiefdom. Seeing the destruction caused by the Thirty Years' War inspired the Prussians to reform and strengthen their military and economy. Then, in 1657, the Duchy of Prussia gained its independence from the Polish Crown, giving free rein to the Hohenzollerns, at least in that region. As they continued to grow in strength, the rulers of Brandenburg-Prussia used the legal independence of Prussia to proclaim themselves kings in 1701. At that moment, King Frederick I of Prussia managed to convince Habsburg Emperor Leopold I to confirm his title, though it was phrased "king in Prussia" rather than "king of Prussia," as Leopold wanted it to be clear that the rest of Frederick's domain still lay under imperial rule. Over the next several decades, Prussia, which began shedding the Brandenburg part of its name, continued to expand its military might. This was best encapsulated by a late 18th-century French politician who said, "Prussia is not a state with an army, but an army with a state."

By the 1740s, the Prussians were powerful enough to directly challenge the Habsburgs. Under the energetic leadership of Frederick II (also known as Frederick the Great; r.1740–1786), they waged two short wars against Habsburgian domains, which were a part of the larger European conflict known as the War of the Austrian Succession (1740–1748). During that confrontation, the Prussians allied with the French, while the Habsburgs were aided by the British, with several other minor allies on both sides. For the first time, Prussia showcased its power, securing several victories and a major expansion by conquering the rich province of Silesia, a region in what is today southwestern Poland. When the Seven Years' War came, the alliances changed. Prussia sided with the British, while the Habsburg monarchy partnered with their former bitter enemy France. Such reversal of roles highlights a significant change in Franco-German relations. From then on, Prussia was the dominant German state, now colliding with France for dominance in Europe. Furthermore, the Habsburgs' grip over the Holy Roman Empire had weakened. They relied almost exclusively on their Austrian domain and, in part, on Bohemia (modern-day Czech Republic), while other Germanic states remained somewhat of an unorganized mess. They were only formally united as a single entity.

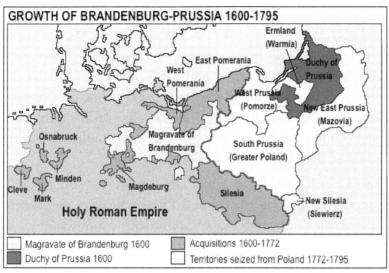

GROWTH OF BRANDENBURG-PRUSSIA 1600-1795

Ermland (Warmia), East Pomerania, West Pomerania, Duchy of Prussia, West Prussia (Pomorze), New East Prussia (Mazovia), Osnabruck, Magravate of Brandenburg, South Prussia (Greater Poland), Minden, Cleve, Mark, Magdeburg, Silesia, New Silesia (Siewierz), Holy Roman Empire

Magravate of Brandenburg 1600
Duchy of Prussia 1600
Acquisitions 1600-1772
Territories seized from Poland 1772-1795

Map of Prussian expansion (top) and a portrait of King Frederick II (bottom). Source: https://commons.wikimedia.org

The final years of the 18th century once again exhibited that France and Germany, or in this case Prussia, were linked as opposites. While France remained on a downward spiral, with internal social issues tearing up the country, Prussia continued to rise. During the 1770s, it took part in the First Partition of Poland, together with Russia and the Habsburgs, most notably accruing so-called West Prussia on the Baltic coast. With that, Prussia managed to connect its Brandenburg provinces with Prussia proper. The Second and Third Partitions came during the 1790s, during which time Poland lost all of its territories. However, Prussia gained control over the Podlachia and Masovia provinces, including Warsaw, which was south of Prussia proper. While the Kingdom of Prussia was expanding, the French monarchy crumbled in 1789 due to the eruption of the French Revolution, culminating with the formation of the First French Republic in 1792.

The French Revolution and the treatment of Louis XVI prompted both the Habsburgs and Prussia to react, issuing threats to the revolutionaries. Such a response was to be expected, as the spreading of revolutionary ideas was a threat to all crowned heads in Europe. France's retort to the threat was a declaration of war. Over the next three years, the war raged on with shifting fortunes, while the list of French enemies grew, eventually including Spain, Portugal, and Britain. However, by 1795, Prussia had enough of the costly war that brought no gains. Thus, a separate peace was signed, allowing it to focus on the Third Partition of Poland. The Habsburgs forged on, this time allied with the British. The major zones of confrontations were northern Italy and the lands of the Holy Roman Empire. After several more years of struggles, both the Habsburgs (1801) and Britain (1802) asked for peace, while France emerged as the victor from the decade-long war. Yet, the ultimate result of the French Revolutionary Wars was the rise of Napoleon, as he seized control over the republic in 1799 through a coup.

Napoleon's rise brought a change to French policies, both internal and external. On the one hand, Napoleon quickly showed his autocratic tendencies, slowly working his way to becoming an emperor in 1804. Nevertheless, France officially retained the title of a republic, as the nation was dubbed a republic until 1809. More importantly, Napoleon was an ambitious and capable commander. His grandiose plans included an expansion of French power; thus, the wars he waged were no longer defensive ones, as they had been in the times of the French Revolution. He led France into a European-wide offensive. In their efforts to contain him, other European powers formed a coalition against France in 1803, with Britain, Russia, the Habsburgs, Naples, and Sweden as members. While Britain had some success on the seas, with a notable win at Trafalgar (1805), the continental war was going in Napoleon's favor. Most notable was his victory over joint Russian and Austrian troops at Austerlitz (1805). Not only did this force the Habsburgs to withdraw from the alliance and seek a separate peace, but this was also the moment the Holy Roman Empire began its final fall.

First, in July 1806, Napoleon signed separate treaties with sixteen Germanic states that were part of the empire. They formally withdrew from the Holy Roman Empire and formed the Confederation of the Rhine. The Habsburgs weren't pleased, but Napoleon's ultimatum led Emperor Francis II to proclaim the final dissolution of the Holy Roman Empire in August 1806, ending almost a millennium-long history of that state. Francis became the emperor of Austria, while other smaller Germanic states flocked to the confederation. Napoleon created it mainly as a military alliance and a buffer to the eastern enemies of France. It signaled a major transgression of French power over Germany, as France penetrated deeper into Germanic lands than ever before. It was especially shocking for the Prussians, who had remained outside the confederation, as now France contested their leadership among the Germans.

Painting of Napoleon (top) and a map of the French Empire and its satellite states in 1812, including the newly formed Confederation of the Rhine (bottom). Source: https://commons.wikimedia.org

The Napoleonic Wars continued over the next several years, with Prussia and Austria attempting to challenge France on several occasions. Yet, they were defeated multiple times, losing parts of their territories as a result. The French took western parts of Prussia and formed the Kingdom of Westphalia, while Austria lost Carinthia, Carniola, its Adriatic ports, and Galicia. Some of those went under direct French rule, while other territories were ceded to French allies in Germany. Nonetheless, Napoleon's rule began to chafe the local Germans, while the continued struggle against the French continued to shape the shared Germanic identity among the population. It mattered little that many Germans were on opposite sides of the battlefield. As the French power began to stretch thin and began to suffer losses, Napoleon's Germanic allies started to abandon him. After the so-called Battle of the Nations (1813), many left the confederation, and it crumbled without French support. Soon, Napoleon suffered his final defeats in 1814 and 1815. Europe was finally at peace.

The future of Europe was decided in the Congress of Vienna (1815). There, all major nations, including the defeated France, now ruled by the old Bourbon dynasty, came together to hammer out the European political landscape after Napoleon's defeat. Of course, France lost most of its expansive gains, while many nations were created and incorporated into other nations. For example, a shortly revived Duchy of Warsaw (Poland) was once again divided between Russia and Prussia. More importantly for the tale of Franco-Germanic relations was the fate of the region that was once the Holy Roman Empire. Prussia regained its lost territories while also receiving Swedish Pomerania, Saxony, and the city of Danzig. The Habsburgs mostly regained their lost lands. Other minor German states had their territorial gains under Napoleon officially recognized. Yet, perhaps most important was the fact that the Holy Roman Empire wasn't revived. Instead, a new German Confederation was formed, covering most of the former Holy

Roman Empire. It was comprised of more than forty independent entities in a loose alliance under Austrian guidance.

From then on, two major things influenced the further development of the German nation. Due to the spurred nationalistic feelings, the idea of German unification began to spread across the Germanic states, or at least among their elites. This was intertwined with the growing competition between Prussia and Austria for the leadership role of the Germanic world. The Prussians were eager to utilize the rise of these nationalistic ideas of unification, while the Austrians opposed it. The Habsburgs realized that Austrian integration into a purely Germanic state was largely incompatible with their empire, which was compromised of numerous European nations, like Hungarians, Czechs, Serbs, and Croats. On the other hand, the Prussians felt that unification could be done under their leadership. The first step they made was the creation of a customs union (the Zollverein) in 1818. It was a commercial alliance that helped the growth of German and Prussian industries and economy. By the mid-1830s, it encompassed most of the Germanic states, but the Prussians were careful to exclude the Austrians from it.

Lifting the trade barriers did more than just strengthen the economic expansion of the Germanic states, which began rapid industrialization in the 1840s. It also further facilitated the growing feeling of a shared German identity. All the while, France went through a period of ups and downs. Its economy and power rose but not as fast as in the Germanic states, while its political and social life was unstable, to say the least. In 1830, a coup led to a change on the throne. King Charles X was replaced by Louis Philippe, a member of a Bourbon dynasty side-branch. This change came as a response to the unwavering autocracy of Charles. Thus, Louis was supposed to be a "citizen king," whose power rested on the bourgeoisie. This change was evident by the fact that his title was "King of the French," not of France. The French monarchy was certainly feeling the repercussions of the revolution.

However, as time went by, this "citizen king" also turned toward authoritarianism to preserve his reign, leading France into further turmoil. It exploded in 1848, as the workers and lower classes remained unsatisfied with the regime. With a new revolution, the monarchy was once again overthrown, and the Second Republic was formed. By the end of the year, Louis Napoleon Bonaparte, Napoleon's nephew, emerged as its president and leader of "all the people." While France was going through yet another revolution and internal upheaval, this time, the rebellious sentiment bubbled over to other nations as well. As such, it became known as the Springtime of Nations or the Revolutions of 1848, as people across the world rebelled. Both Prussia and Austria were affected but in very different ways.

The Prussians rebelled against the absolute monarchy of King Friedrich Wilhelm IV (Frederick William; r. 1840–1861), leading to some concessions on his part. Despite that, there were major demonstrations and even casualties. Around Prussia and among other minor Germanic states, most protests and uprisings were actually aimed at promoting German unification alongside demands for liberal reforms, as it was seen as the logical next step toward a better life. This caused a crisis for the German Confederation, as many wanted more direct elections and participation. The upheaval culminated with a new National Assembly, which directly offered King Friedrich the crown of a united Germany. He refused, as it was too radical a step for him. By late 1849, the revolutionary tide in Germany was broken by local princes and dukes, often through immense violence. Nevertheless, the signaled support for German unity didn't go unnoticed.

An 1850 map of Europe. Source: https://commons.wikimedia.org

Farther south, the Austrian Habsburgs were faced with more ominous threats, as pretty much all non-Germanic nationalities under their rule revolted, asking for more autonomy. The crisis was so strong that Emperor Ferdinand I abdicated in favor of his more liberal nephew, Franz Joseph. Even worse, the empire was embroiled in a conflict that resembled a civil war, as the various rebellions and nationalities clashed against each other, sometimes even in favor of the Habsburgs, as the people hoped to gain some favor. In the end, peace was restored, yet the Austrians were still too preoccupied with domestic affairs to influence the affairs of the German Confederation to any significant degree. As the dust continued to settle, most of the Germanic states, including Prussia and Austria, returned to their conservative ways since the results of the uprisings proved fleeting. At the same time, the Austro-Prussian rivalry was reheating once again.

The French Republic went through a similar path. Louis Napoleon Bonaparte quietly and steadily regrouped his positions and power, with the country slowly descending into a new autocracy. By 1852, he decided to "promote" himself from president to emperor, becoming known as Emperor Napoleon III, once again transforming the republic into an empire. This transformation went largely unchallenged. With this move, France was once more looking to prove its dominant position in Europe. The revival of such imperial politics sent France on a collision course with Prussia, which continued its rise as a European power and the center of German unification.

Chapter 2 – Enemies at the Borders: Immediate Causes for the War

While there were enmities between the French and the Germans, intertwined with their long-running struggle for dominance over continental Europe, those were not the immediate causes for the war between France and Prussia. They did facilitate it, in a long line of cause and effect, but the direct origin of the conflict began to arise only during the 1850s.

By 1852, Napoleon III had established himself as the new French emperor, and he was filled with dreams of grandeur. During his reign, especially in the early years, France exhibited internal stability with signs of economic growth and gradual industrialization. Such a position allowed him to pursue his ideas of glory in foreign affairs. Napoleon III wanted to return France to the forefront of the world powers and gain the same kind of respect and prestige his uncle had. He had some success, as he expanded the French colonial domain in Indochina and Africa, strengthened French control over Algeria, and made a foothold in China, alongside other colonial powers. However, these successes seemed minor when compared with his failures in Europe. During the Crimean War (1854–1856), he sided with the victorious British and Ottoman forces against Imperial Russia, yet that expedition yielded only expenses without any palpable gains. Then, in 1859, he turned his gaze closer to home, deciding to support the Italian Kingdom of Piedmont in their war to expel the Austrians from the Apennine Peninsula. His goal was to expand French influence over what he hoped to become a loose Italian confederation.

An 1855 portrait of Napoleon III (top) and a depiction of the French presence in Algeria (bottom). Source: https://commons.wikimedia.org

Initially, it seemed Napoleon's plans might succeed, as joint Italo-French forces won against the Habsburgs, prompting them to ask for peace within a few months. France gained some land in northern Italy, mainly around Milan. These were exchanged with Piedmont for areas around Nice and Savoy. Despite achieving territorial gains, Napoleon's plans quickly turned sour. After two years of conflicts and struggles, Piedmont expanded across the peninsula, leaving only the papacy in Rome and the Austrians in Venice. Instead of a loose confederation, by early 1861, France had gained a unified Kingdom of Italy as its southern neighbor. To make matters worse for Napoleon, he suffered further diplomatic failures in North America. His politics almost dragged France into the US Civil War (1861–1865), while his attempt to secure Mexico under French influence failed miserably. The expedition forces sent to secure a puppet ruler in 1861 fought against the Mexicans for six years before being defeated in 1867. The French ruler in Mexico was executed, France was humiliated, and Napoleon lost many of his supporters. Instead of bringing peace and prosperity, he brought wars that ended mostly in losses or empty victories and financial debacles. To make matters worse, his erratic foreign policy alienated most French allies, leaving her alone on the world stage.

While France seemed to be on a downward spiral, Prussia's fate appeared to follow a different trajectory. Although Napoleon III enjoyed a promising start, Friedrich Wilhelm IV led Prussia through a rocky period in the 1850s. He had to sort out political instability caused by the Revolutions of 1848 while continuing to expand the economy and industry. Prussian weakness, especially on the diplomatic front, was highlighted throughout the decade. First, it suffered a defeat against Denmark in the First Schleswig War (1848–1851), which was more the result of international pressure than its failures on the battlefield. Furthermore, other great powers marginalized Prussia during the Crimean War (1854–1856) and the Italian War (1859). With that, its status as a European power became an issue going into the 1860s.

Such developments didn't sit particularly well with Friedrich's younger brother, Wilhelm (William), who became a regent when the king suffered a stroke. His plan to return Prussian status to its former glory rested on expanding its military might. Wilhelm sprang into action in 1861 when he became the king after the death of his older brother. Such expenditures caused some backlash among the Prussian politicians. Amidst the crisis, King Wilhelm I considered abdicating but instead appointed Otto von Bismarck as the prime minister in September of 1862. This proved to a crucial turning point for Prussia. At the time, Bismarck wasn't a prominent or very experienced politician. His career was mostly in foreign affairs, serving first as the Prussian representative in the assembly of the German Confederation and then as an ambassador in Russia and France. Wilhelm chose him only after Minister of War Albrecht von Roon advised him to do so. Nevertheless, Bismarck quickly proved his worth, as he managed to outmaneuver opponents of the military reforms.

A perfect storm was formed in the political and military leadership of Prussia. King Wilhelm, an old general who believed that political power lay in the nation's military, was supported by Bismarck, who believed that Prussia's ultimate goal must be the unification of Germany through "blood and iron." Roon, believing in the necessity of military reforms, bridged the gap between politics and the army. Finally, the Prussian chief of staff was famous Field Marshal Helmuth von Moltke, who personally led the reorganization and restructuring of the Prussian forces. Moltke observed the advances of other European nations during the 1850s, realizing that the Prussian military had to expand in number, adopt new types of arms, master quicker and better mobilization, improve communication and deployment using modern technologies, and create a professional and well-trained officer core. By 1864, Prussia, under Bismarck's leadership, was prepared to showcase its newfound strength.

Its first opponent was Denmark, a perfect target to readdress Prussian frustration from the Schleswig War. A change on the Danish throne in 1863 opened up territorial disputes over the territories of Schleswig and Holstein, provinces that were populated mostly by Germans. They were officially part of the German Confederation but were under Danish reign. The new Danish monarch issued a new constitution, which proclaimed Schleswig as an integral part of the Danish Crown, violating the peace treaty from the 1850s. That gave Bismarck enough pretext to launch a campaign, utilizing German nationalist sentiment to further legitimize the Prussian attack. It was enough to bring the rest of the confederation, including the Austrians, to join in to defend the German people. More importantly, other major powers remained largely uninterested in the conflict, with only Britain showing mild support to the Danes. In the end, the combined forces of the German states outnumbered and outgunned the Danish forces, conquering almost all of Denmark by mid-1864. By October, a peace treaty had been signed. Austria gained Holstein, while Prussia gained Schleswig and recognition of its strength.

An 1857 photo of Wilhelm I (top) and an 1860s illustration of Bismarck, Roon, and Moltke in said order (bottom). Source: https://commons.wikimedia.org

After the quick victory, Austria and Prussia agreed to form joint sovereignty over the two provinces, as they were historically seen as a single entity. Expectedly, this created numerous issues between the two nations, leading some historians to assume it was all done according to Bismarck's grand design. Such claims are debatable, to say the least, yet Bismarck's ability to adapt to new situations and use them to his and Prussia's advantage remains undisputed. By early 1866, tensions had risen enough for the Prussians to accuse the Austrians of breaching the joint sovereignty by allowing Holstein to organize an assembly. Mutual accusations were exchanged, leading both sides to look for allies. Bismarck secured an alliance with Italy, as it wanted to liberate Venice from the Habsburgs, while Austria found support from the other German states, which feared Prussian military might. Both sides began concentrating troops on the borders, issuing mobilization orders. War was clearly imminent.

Napoleon III was also interested in the development of the Austro-Prussian crisis. He met with Bismarck in late 1865, assuring him that France would stay neutral in the case of war. It seems that Napoleon believed that a conflict between the German states would only exhaust them, allowing him to gain political concessions for France and even enlarge it. However, neutrality was all that Bismarck and Prussia needed. By May 1866, both sides were geared up for war. In the early days of June, Austrians brought the issues to the assembly of the German Confederation while also preparing for the gathering of the Holstein Diet. The Prussians then proclaimed their agreement with Austria was void and invaded Holstein, while the German Confederation responded with a partial mobilization. Instead of intimidating them, this prompted the Prussians to declare that the German Confederation was dissolved. Their army invaded Saxony, Hesse, and Hanover, with Italy also declaring war on Austria.

Since the Prussian Army was reformed and modernized, it quickly dissolved any Austrian hopes of a swift victory and simultaneously crumbled all of Napoleon's plans. Prussia managed to defeat the Hanoverian forces by the end of June and also amassed troops near Moravia (modern-day Czech Republic), where the Austrians were gathering their forces. Two large armies met in the Battle of Königgrätz (present-day Sadová) on July 3rd. The Prussians exhibited technological and tactical supremacy, leaving the Austrian army running from the battlefield in shreds. While they continued to advance through the Czech Republic and Slovakia, other Prussian troops defeated Saxon and Bavarian troops. The Austrians, knowing they were facing total defeat, asked for peace on July 22nd, ending the war in a mere seven weeks. A few days later, on August 12th, the Italians were forced to end their campaign as well, though their struggle seemed a bit more even, as both sides achieved some victories.

After Moltke and the Prussian Army achieved victory on the battlefield, it was up to Bismarck to capitalize on it. In fact, he was in favor of accepting a quick defeat from the Austrians without pursuing further gains. As a keen politician and diplomat, Bismarck knew that if Prussia pushed too far, Russia or France might intervene. Furthermore, he wanted to avoid too much revanchism from Austria or other Germanic states. The peace was ratified in Prague in late August but not without French interference. Prussia annexed Schleswig, Holstein, Hanover, Hesse-Kassel, Nassau, and Frankfurt, while the rest of the northern Germanic states were organized into the North German Confederation. Through this confederation, Prussia basically controlled their military and foreign relations; these states were basically just a step away from annexation. In trying to prevent the further unification of Germanic states under Prussia, Napoleon demanded Bismarck's assurance of independence for Saxony, Bavaria, Württemberg, Baden, and Hesse-Darmstadt. By early October, Italy had managed to secure Venice, though it was first handed over to France, which then transferred it to Italy. This was done to save Austrian face, for they claimed to have won their war with Italy.

The Peace of Prague also meant that the Habsburgs were excluded from German affairs and matters of unification. The merger was to encompass only so-called Lesser Germany (*Kleindeutschland*), not Austria or any other Habsburgian lands. Despite that, France was still threatened. Instead of having a loose confederation that was exhausted by war, Napoleon was faced with the strong North German Confederation, which was basically an enlarged Prussia. It had a population of thirty million, compared to France's thirty-eight million, with a much more developed industry. Furthermore, due to military reforms, Prussia had an army roughly one-third larger than France. If Prussia was to spread to the southern Germanic states, below the River Mein, not only would it gain a substantial boost in population and the economy but also a strategic advantage against the French. Attacking on the wide front from Luxembourg to Switzerland would allow them to easily flank French defenses. Thus, preventing German unification became one of the paramount goals of Napoleon's politics.

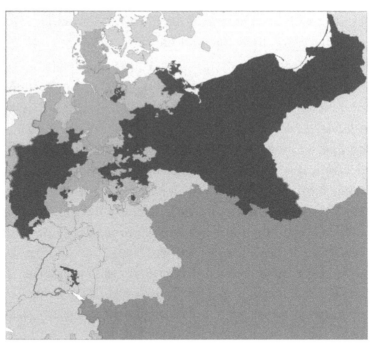

Map of the Austro-Prussian War of 1866—Austrian Empire (red), Austrian allies (pink), Prussian allies (light blue), Prussia (dark blue), Prussia acquisitions (cyan), and neutral states (green). Source: https://commons.wikimedia.org

Soon after the dust had settled, Napoleon tried to buy Luxembourg, which was at the time under a personal union with the Netherlands, ruled by King William III. William was in debt, and Napoleon sought to improve both his position in France and France's position in Europe. An added bonus was that Luxembourg was a rather important strategic fortification between France and Prussia. Napoleon hoped that Bismarck wouldn't object to it, as it was supposedly part of their oral agreement made before the Austro-Prussian War. It seems that Bismarck hinted at having no objection to French hegemony in Belgium and Luxembourg if France remained neutral. However, by early 1867, Prussia was in a position to object to French expansion. All of a sudden, Bismarck stopped playing the role of Napoleon's malleable protégé concerned about French reactions. Instead, his political posturing was one of dominance and power, as he threatened with war if France went through with the purchase. Instead of war, a conference of major powers was held in London, with the final result being the independence of Luxembourg guaranteed by those nations.

Nevertheless, tensions remained high as both sides were on the brink of war. Yet, it seems that neither of them was prepared to stake their bets. Napoleon realized that France needed to modernize its military if it was to challenge the Prussians on the battlefield. Bismarck was concerned that another war might unify other major powers against Prussia, as they were sure to feel threatened by its rising power. Instead, he decided to bide his time while preparing the stage for a final reckoning with France. Using his keen political skills, Bismarck leaned on Napoleon's posturing. This made France seem more powerful than it was while also showing it as a possible threat due to its publicized interest in taking control of Belgium, Luxembourg, and even the Rhineland. In the eyes of the other powers, it started to look like France was a much bigger threat than the enlarged Prussia. Playing on that, Bismarck went on to work on isolating France from acquiring possible allies against Prussia.

In 1868, Bismarck once again taunted the French. He formed an all-German customs parliament, or *Zollparlament*, strengthening Prussian ties with the southern Germanic states. Of course, this irked Napoleon, and he reminded Prussia of his previous demands for the independence of those Germanic countries. He even prolonged summer military maneuvers in hopes of being taken more seriously. This worked for Bismarck. Once again, it was France that seemed threatening, as Prussia was far from able to absorb the southern states peacefully. Their rulers were keen on maintaining their sovereignty despite wanting an eased trade with Prussia. Napoleon's posturing was also working in favor for Bismarck internally. The possible French invasion only heated up German nationalistic feelings, which was especially important in the southern states. As time passed, despite the upper classes remaining adamant in retaining political independence, their citizens slowly began favoring a unified nation state. This was a reality that could only be attained through Prussia.

While the two nations remained in what could be described as a diplomatic stare-down, both Napoleon and Bismarck faced issues at home. The French, or at least the urban elite, began voicing their displeasure with the emperor's politics. They deplored his rather authoritarian constitution. The economy also began to show signs of distress. The expenses of Napoleon's various adventures, from Mexico to Italy, began to catch up, and even the latest military reforms demanded a substantial investment. Furthermore, his own extravagant lifestyle and leeching entourage worsened the emperor's image among the masses. In an attempt to secure his shaken rule, Napoleon called for an election in 1869, hoping his candidates would win through political trickery. However, even with ballot stuffing, gerrymandering, and other similar tactics, the opposition managed to secure 25 percent of the seats in the assembly. In reality, the opposition was much closer to 50 percent, prompting massive protests and demonstrations. Urban factory workers even began demanding a "red revolution" and a new republic. The emperor was prepared to use violence to break these efforts, but he instead chose a softer approach. Attempting to appease the protestors, he relaxed his authoritarian reign and put an eminent liberal reformer, Émile Ollivier, in the position of prime minister. Despite that, France remained rather divided and troubled. The only thing that all the French could agree upon was supporting the conflict with Prussia, as it was a matter of national pride.

On the other side of the border, Bismarck also ran into domestic troubles. In the Prussian assembly, he had to fight both the liberals, who wanted to reduce the size and expenditure of the military, and the conservatives, who opposed new laws and taxes. Furthermore, he had to wrestle with other Germanic governments and the confederation assembly. Making matters even worse, Bismarck also faced the issue of the rising industrial working class, which was permeated with socialist ideals. His goals of unification were additionally complicated by the fact that the southern Germanic states began leaning away from Prussia; they even began thinking about asking for French protection in the case of war. The northern states also began to question Prussian leadership to a degree. Bismarck's position was further shaken by numerous local national liberals who thought he was taking too much time to unify the states. While the elites and politicians were strung all over the political scale, the common population started to grow tired of the complicated system of overlapping assemblies and constant elections. Stagnation and discouragement began to spread when it came to matters of unification. Thus, while Napoleon favored war as a means of securing his reign, Bismarck saw the conflict as a crude tool that would remove rising obstacles to the German union.

The gunpowder kegs were aligned; all that was needed was a proper spark. The first one came in early 1870 when there was a rumor of the North German Confederation assembly offering King Wilhelm the title of Kaiser, or emperor. Both Wilhelm and Bismarck seemed in favor of such a development, yet Napoleon vocally threatened with war. In the end, the matter never moved further toward actualization. Soon afterward, another spark was deliberately set by Bismarck. He, or rather Prussia, invested in a railway through Switzerland, connecting Italy and the Germanic states. When such a subtle hint went unnoticed, Bismarck gave a well-measured speech. Without sounding aggressive or threatening, he hinted at an existence of a Prusso-Italian alliance aimed at France, which would be facilitated by said railway link. The French public once again cried for blood, yet the issue didn't evolve any further. Napoleon and his government remained surprisingly passive and inert. While Bismarck worked on isolating France, Napoleon's foreign minister just stood by watching. For example, by

1870, Italy no longer felt fidelity to Napoleon, despite France waging a costly war in 1859 on its behalf.

Realizing that his government needed more active and forceful diplomacy, Napoleon III appointed Duke Antoine Agénorde Gramont as his minister of foreign relations. Gramont saw himself as Bismarck's match, promising he would manufacture a conflict on whatever excuse arose first. He wanted to teach Prussia a lesson and dismantle its position that had been gained in 1866. Prime Minister Ollivier agreed, stating that the next disrespectful action from Bismarck and Prussia must lead to war. At the time, sixty-two-year-old Napoleon was ill and unable to involve himself more directly in the decision-making process, yet his appointed ministers were set on the warpath. Little did they know that they were walking straight into Bismarck's trap, one he had been preparing since September of 1869. The Spanish Parliament then offered their crown to Leopold Hohenzollern, Wilhelm's cousin. Besides recognizing the rise of Prussia through such a choice, Leopold had other benefits as well. He looked like a versatile and prestigious candidate.

Despite sounding like quite an offer, both Leopold and Wilhelm initially rejected it. Spain was unstable and in search of a new royal house since it had deposed the old Bourbon dynasty in 1868. If Leopold was to be chased off, it would bring shame to the entire Hohenzollern dynasty. However, Bismarck saw an opportunity there, and in May of 1870, he enticed Leopold's father to accept in his name. A few weeks later, Leopold himself agreed. By early July, the news had reached France, prompting an immediate fiery response. All of France was gearing up for war, for if the Spanish throne went to the Hohenzollerns, they would be encircled and their position weakened beyond repair. It seemed both Bismarck and Gramont would get their war. Yet, Wilhelm was worried that he'd seem like an instigator. Thus, without discussing it with his chancellor, he persuaded Leopold and his father to reject the offer, which they did on July 11th. It seemed that the crisis would be averted, which possibly seemed like a sign of weakness in Gramont's eyes.

Despite achieving a diplomatic victory, Gramont wasn't satisfied. Since he was denied an opportunity to settle the score through war, he wanted to humiliate the Prussians. It is also significant to note that he wasn't alone in the sentiment, as most of the French public and political elite seemed thirsty for war. Pushing his fortunes, Gramont sent a telegram to the French ambassador in Prussia, demanding a public and written renunciation from Wilhelm I, as well as a pledge that Prussia would never reach for the Spanish Crown. The ambassador met with the king on July 13th at Bad Ems, a spa, where Wilhelm was on a summer retreat. The Prussian king listened to the demand, then abruptly walked away without a word. He immediately sent a dispatch to Bismarck in Berlin. The message from Ems arrived while the chancellor was despondent about his plans crumbling. As he read about the events in Ems, Bismarck's calculated and unscrupulous political mind immediately saw an opportunity.

A later illustration of the Ems meeting between King Wilhelm I (left) and the French ambassador (right). Source: https://commons.wikimedia.org

While keeping the original meaning of the message, Bismarck reworded part of it to sound as if the king was rude toward the ambassador, emphasizing that he refused him an audience after the initial talk. At the same time, he stressed that the French demand was insulting to Wilhelm. Then he circulated the message through newspapers across Europe. For Bismarck's plan to work, he needed France to make the first move. The so-called Ems Dispatch became the perfect red flag for the "Gallic bull." The undiplomatic wording of the meeting between the ambassador and the king was publicized on July 14th, adding insult to injury as it was Bastille Day, a national holiday in France. For Gramont and the agitated French, it was a gauntlet across the face. By the next day, France had ordered mobilization, followed by the Prussians and other Germanic states. After a few days spent in serving bureaucratic necessities, on July 19th, France declared war on Prussia. Finally, both Bismarck and Gramont got the war for which they yearned.

In the end, on the grand scale of things, the Franco-Prussian War began because of the long-lasting competition between the French and the Germans, as the European balance of power was tipping. One side wanted to retain its superiority, while the other wanted to become the dominant power. A pinnacle of that struggle was the issue of German unification, which was undoubtedly a tilting moment in history. However, when seen from a more immediate and closer historical perspective, it was a war that was sparked by the political needs of leaders in both France and Prussia. Both nations had internal issues and fractures that a war could mend through the power of unifying nationalism. Finally, the war was avoidable, especially when considering that the final crisis that ignited the gunpowder keg was quite frivolous on its own.

Chapter 3 – Two Fighters in the Ring: Prussian and French Armies, Tactics, and Organization

To understand the course of the war, we must first get acquainted with the state of both the French and the Prussian forces. The most common depiction is one of Prussian superiority, where the Germans were professional soldiers equipped with modern weaponry, while the French were a ragtag mass waging war with outdated guns. The reality is, of course, much more complicated than that.

The first issue that needs to be addressed is the matter of numbers, showcasing the first of several major differences between the two warring sides. On one side was France, which had a larger standing army, roughly 400,000 strong. The proposed reforms were supposed to swell that number up to roughly 800,000, but they were incomplete by 1870. Thus, on the brink of the war, the French headquarters counted on about 500,000 men, who were conscripted in about three weeks. Furthermore, the proposed reforms were supposed to form local militia units named *Garde Mobile*, a territorial defense made up of non-drafted able-bodied men who would have some limited military training. These troops weren't ready at all in 1870, numbering only about 100,000 conscripts, and their fighting capabilities and deployment speed were questionable at best.

The Prussians, or to be more precise, the North German Federation as a whole, had a smaller standing army, around 300,000 strong. However, it had a much deeper well of reserves and their own militia, the *Landwehr*, which would increase its fighting strength to just shy of one million men. Furthermore, the south Germanic states could field another 200,000. However, the Prussian high command believed their southern allies might not join in, despite secret military agreements that had been signed in the years prior to the war. The discrepancies in the strength of the two warring sides are mostly accountable by the different organizations and drafting systems of the armies, with Prussia favoring wider conscription. Yet, it is also vital to mention that by the second half of the 19th century, France was becoming an older nation with a lower reproduction rate. This meant that every generation would produce fewer soldiers than the one before. Regardless, it was clear that the Germans had numerical superiority, at least on paper, yet those numbers in the end also depended upon the speed of mobilization and deployment.

When seeing these rough numbers, common sense dictates that the French should have been more worried about their position on the battlefield. This wasn't so, mostly due to the slight hubris of the commanding officers. Many of them reckoned that the French were more professional, as the conscripted soldiers served at least seven years and were given incentives for reenlisting. Thus, by 1870, roughly half of the French soldiers had been in active service for more than seven years. In comparison, the Prussian soldiers had three years of active duty, followed by four years as reserves, and then another five in the *Landwehr*. Thus, at least on paper, the French were professionals, while the Prussian Army was one of reservists. However, the reality was vastly different. According to accounts left by some French officers, instead of having professional and experienced troops, they often had men in their fifties or sixties, men who were jaded and cynical and often more focused on drinking in the barracks than on practicing their military skills. To make matters worse, when a fresh batch of recruits came along, they often got dragged into the ways of their elders and quickly lost their vigor.

Prussian soldiers on a march in autumn of 1870. Source:
https://commons.wikimedia.org

In contrast, the Prussian Army seemed more fit and better trained, at least in theory. During their three years of primary service, they would undergo severe physical training, coupled with numerous theoretical lectures and stories of veterans. Furthermore, it has been said that the Prussians did more target practice shooting than any other army in Europe. Yet, the training wasn't only focused on military skills and knowledge. The officers, pretty much the only professional soldiers in the army, also worked on instilling their men with ethics, discipline, and morals, promoting the spirit of defending the fatherland. At first glance, it would seem that the Prussians were more than superior in this regard, yet their system did have substantial drawbacks. Despite their ferocious training, by 1870, not many of their troops ever witnessed actual combat, even in the reserves. Most of the French soldiers took part in at least one campaign. Moreover, they too had a desire to teach the Germans a lesson, which gave them ample fighting spirits, at least in the barracks.

There was also another jarring difference between the two armies in terms of their education. The French tended to demean their foes, calling the Prussians an "army of lawyers." Despite their intentions to insult, this illustrates the fact that most Prussian soldiers had some form of basic education and literacy, thanks to compulsory primary schools. It allowed them to have a much better comprehension of maps and complicated tactical maneuvers, among other things. Like in everyday life, having an education meant having an easier understanding of what was going on. On the other hand, most of the French soldiers were uncultured and illiterate. This was partially caused by the lack of compulsory education but also due to how the draft system functioned. Unlike Germany, which pretty much made every able-bodied man enlist, the French drew a lottery every year. However, it was possible to buy out the enlistment for only 2,400 francs, something a bourgeois elite could easily pay. Even poor peasant families were sometimes able to scrape that amount up to keep their men at home. Nevertheless, with the upper classes pretty much avoiding the service, much of the French Army was made up of uneducated rural folk.

The level of education posed another problem for the French military at the time, as the majority of officers were drawn from conscription. The low wages and pensions offered little incentive even for the middle classes, let alone the elites. Thus, the same societal dregs that made up the recruits eventually made it to the officer's ranks, at least the junior ones. Their lack of education made them perfect for executing orders but not too viable for thinking on their own and assuming responsibility for the command over their troops. Even worse, the pace of advancing in the French Army was slow, sometimes taking a whole decade to earn a rank, leaving many of the junior officers in their fifties or even sixties. Such a system, altogether, provided lower-ranked officers who were often intellectually blank, physically unfit, and plagued with apathy and inertia. According to a French contemporary, they were best at keeping their mouths shut and getting numb in a tavern or café. This, of course, wasn't the case with the higher ranks, which consisted of educated elites, but they were instead beset by petty rivalries, jealousy, and favoritism.

Their Prussian counterparts, when it comes to the senior ranked officers, often shared those erosive traits as well. It was seemingly unavoidable, as these men were proud members of the elites whose egos were large enough to fill a room. However, unlike the French, who did little to deal with such faulty personalities, Moltke actively combated it through reassignments or outright dismissals. His commanders had to be cooperative at least to a minimum degree. Yet, the true difference in the officer corps was more striking in the lower ranks. The Prussian officers were often drawn from middle-class recruits, thus often having more than just basic education, and they were enticed to pursue their military careers through a much quicker advancement through the ranks. This meant Prussian junior officers were often much younger, fit, and more capable than their French counterparts. To further convince them to stay in the army, those officers were offered government sinecure as well as hefty pensions after retiring from the army. Nevertheless, their active wages remained mediocre.

A picture of Moltke circa 1870 (top) and an illustration of Prussian officers honing their skills through wargames (bottom). Source: https://commons.wikimedia.org

These differences also created a contrast in the organizational aspect of the two armies. Over the course of the 19th century, Prussians created a rather systemic and hierarchical organization of their troops, which differed only slightly between peacetime and war. This was epitomized in the famed *Generalstab*, or Great General Staff, a full-time body that actively worked on maintaining a high degree of preparation, creating plans both for campaigns and mobilizations, and honing military tactics and skills through exercises like wargames. This created a constant baseline in the Prussian Army, making it ready for any contingency. The quality of the Great General Staff was only heightened by the fact that its members were picked solely based on merit and capabilities, ignoring seniority or connections. Members of this highest military body all trained together and learned the same military philosophy, which, at the time, was based on Moltke's vision of the army. This made them interchangeable and reliable. Such training also created a sense of comradery between them. Overall, the *Generalstab* was, as Moltke himself described it, a nervous system of the Prussian military, creating a strong administrative backbone and increasing its functionality.

On the other hand, the French military was much less organized, without an active staff during peacetime. While there was no active conflict, the army organization existed almost entirely on a regimental scale, tasked with creating group morale in a unit. And while the Germans practiced territorial placement of their units and recruits, the French distributed their soldiers without regard to their origins. Above them was a loose organization of various committees and guidelines, with the Ministry of War at its helm. It is worth noting that the French Army was nominally led by Emperor Napoleon III himself, contrasting Moltke's professionalism as the Chief of Staff in Prussia. As it was previously mentioned, while the Prussian command depended upon promoting capable officers, the French high command was a seniority-ridden organization. Thus, overall, the French Army was much more centralized and conservative, steeped in the traditions of the olden days. Some strides toward rectifying this were made in the years prior to the war, with an attempt to create territorial divisions of the army and making promotions based on the emperor's choices. Yet, these military reforms were either not finished or were completely scrapped by the early 1870s.

So far, the description of the two armies leans toward depicting the Prussians as the superior military force. However, it is important to note that the differences may not have been as stark as they might seem at first glance. Up to that point, the French were seen as the primary land force in Europe, with the British commanding the seas. They had a long tradition and showed their worth in numerous wars in the past. For many, they were indeed the favorite in a conflict that seemed inevitable in the eyes of many neutral observers. Furthermore, the balance of power may have tipped the other way if the planned military reforms in France had enough time to be fulfilled. Nevertheless, the French military had a few aces up its sleeves in terms of modern weaponry.

With the outbreak of the war, the main Prussian weapon was the Dreyse needle gun, a breechloading bolt action rifle. It was first introduced in the Prussian Army as far back as 1841, and it performed rather impressively. It had an estimated firing speed of 5 to 6 rounds per minute and an effective range of about 400 to 600 yards (365 to 550 meters), while its maximum range went up to 750 yards (685 meters). It outperformed almost all other guns in use, proving its worth during the war with Denmark and the Habsburgs, who, at the time, still outfitted their troops with muzzle-loading rifles. Its major point of supremacy was its reload speed, as a Prussian soldier fired up to five shots while the Austrian managed to reload his gun once. However, it had several critical issues as well. Its range was far from desirable, and its breech mechanism wasn't perfectly fitted, making the gun lose vital firing pressure, which, in turn, made its shot far less powerful. It was said the Dreyse often inflicted lighter wounds; sometimes, casualties would even get back on their feet and continue fighting.

Prior to 1866, the French military used a muzzle-loading rifle similar to the Austrians. Yet, upon seeing how superior the Dreyse was, they decided to rush the development of a new gun: the Chassepot *Fusil modèle 1866*. Its design was finalized in late 1866 and introduced into service in 1867. The Chassepot was a superior rifle in all aspects. Its effective range was about 1,000 yards (915 meters), with its maximum range reportedly going up to 1,600 yards (1,465 meters). The rate of fire ranged between eight and fifteen rounds per minute. The Chassepot's breechloading mechanism was fitted with rubber seals, making it much more energy efficient. Its caliber was slightly smaller, 11 millimeters (0.433 inches) to 15.4 millimeters (0.61 inches); however, the French bullets were milled and jacketed in linen instead of paper and were also packed with more gunpowder. All of these smaller advantages amounted to higher muzzle velocity, longer range, better precision, and, most impressively, high stopping power. According to pre-war French testing, while the entry wound was still the size of a single bullet, exit wounds were usually seven to thirteen times larger. They caused massive damage to inner organs, bones, and muscle, making every hit a potentially deadly one. If that alone wasn't enough, the Chassepot was slightly shorter and lighter, making it easier for transport and use. Furthermore, its smaller caliber meant that the French soldiers could carry more ammunition than their Prussian counterpart—105 rounds compared to 70.

An 1870s picture of a French soldier with a Chassepot rifle (top) and an 1870 illustration of a mitrailleuse crew (bottom). Source: https://commons.wikimedia.org

Besides the standard issue rifle, the French also developed the Montigny-Reffye mitrailleuse, named after the grapeshot, or *mitraille* in French. It was originally developed by the Belgian engineer Joseph Montigny during the 1850s, before Napoleon III expressed an interest in its concept. Montigny worked with Jean-Baptiste Verchère de Reffye to create the mitrailleuse in 1865. It was an early type of a machine gun, similar to the contemporary Gatling gun, with a number of rifle barrels strapped to an artillery chassis. The original Montigny design used thirty-seven barrels, while the later Montigny-Reffye had twenty-five barrels. The mitrailleuse used a hand-cranked mechanism to transform it into a rapid-firing gun. The cranking mechanism gave it the nickname *moulin à café*, or "coffee grinder." It was breech loaded with cartridges, thus making the overall rate of fire dependent on the skill of the four-man crew operating it. Nevertheless, with an average of one hundred to two hundred rounds per minute, it outgunned any conventional rifle. It also had an effective range of around 1,200 yards (1,100 meters), going up to a maximum of at least 2,000 yards (1,830 meters). During testing, a stray bullet reportedly managed to kill a villager about 3,000 yards (2,740 meters) away. Furthermore, its 13-millimeter (0.512-inch) ammo was packed with twice the amount of gunpowder used by the Chassepot, giving it high muzzle velocity and stopping power.

This novel weapon was initially kept a secret, but eventually, its existence was witnessed by the Prussians. Nonetheless, the German forces didn't have anything comparable in their arsenal, nor were there any signs of attempting to develop a similar rapid-firing gun. Despite seeing its devastating potential, Prussian observers noted that it showed notable vulnerability, as it lacked any shield or cover, making its crew exposed to enemy fire. Its range meant it had to be relatively in the front lines as well, unlike proper artillery. Regardless, both the Chassepot and the mitrailleuse swayed the firepower balance toward the French side, at least on paper. The only armament in which the Prussian had the upper hand was artillery.

The French were using the so-called La Hitte cannons, a muzzle-loaded bored gun that fired shells weighing 4 kilograms (8.8 pounds). It was designed in 1858 and introduced the following year, proving to be a powerful novelty in the war against the Austrians. At the time, bored barrels were a newly implemented technology, allowing the gun to fire heavier projectiles farther. Its maximum range was reported at about 3,280 yards (3,000 meters). However, the French shells used timed fuses, which had only two settings, exploding either at 1,200 yards (1,100 meters) or at 2,500 yards (2,285 meters), making its "kill zones" rather limited, at least when it came to explosive rounds. Regardless, the French seemed satisfied with their artillery and were convinced that it was still competitive on the 1870 battlefield. In contrast, the Prussians faced similar technology against the Austrians in 1866 and realized their old smoothbore cannons were inadequate. Thus, they invested in developing new artillery technology, producing the cutting-edge Krupp six-pounder.

This gun was introduced in between two Prussian wars, and it adopted not only bored barrels but also breechloading technology. Additionally, the cannon itself was made out of steel instead of the bronze used by the French for their guns. All of that made the Krupp fire more accurately, have at least a third longer range, and have a rate of fire that was twice as fast. Further improvements were made in the realm of the shell itself. Despite its name, the weight of Krupp's projectiles was actually 6 kilograms or 13.2 pounds. That, of course, meant a higher destructive power. Finally, the shells were fitted with percussion detonated fuses, making their operational ranges much wider than of the French La Hitte. Both the Krupp and the Chassepot paint a picture of both sides preparing for war and improving upon what they deemed were their weakest points in terms of armament technology. However, artillery deficiency was a

by mending their own tactical disadvantages without waiting for confirmation from the *Generalstab*.

Finally, it is significant to mention that the Prussian military was the first in Europe to utilize modern civilian technologies to its own benefit, most notably railways and the telegraph. Realizing the potential of trains for carrying supplies and troops, the Prussian military diverted its infrastructural spending from fortresses to railways, both private- and state-owned. This created a functional railway network in militarily useful regions, giving them the infrastructure needed for massive troop movements. That sped up both mobilization and deployment of units while easing their resupplying and reinforcements. The French, on the other hand, had substantial issues with their underdeveloped railways, which were almost exclusively in private hands. Any substantial military use required a lot of bureaucratic work to be done. As for the telegraph, Moltke was the first general to fully rely on these electronic messages to relay his orders. This not only sped up the transfer of information and reactions from the General Staff but also allowed simultaneous coordination of much more complicated maneuvers and tactics.

Overall, it is clear that, in most cases, the French and the Prussian forces were almost polar opposites. One side stuck to time-tested traditional military doctrines, while the other went on to innovate and ultimately transform how armies functioned. In hindsight, it is clear whose approach was better, but it is vital to remember that, at the time, not many were so sure, apart from maybe Moltke and his inner circle.

Chapter 4 – The Battle Begins: Initial Positioning and Opening Clashes

Despite both nations being on the verge of war for years, neither was actually immediately prepared for a conflict. Both needed some time to mobilize their troops, as well as time to arm and deploy them. Thus, the principal concern in the early days of the Franco-Prussian War was the speed of mobilization and positioning of soldiers.

For the French, this was a "make or break moment," as they held the early edge. They had a larger active army, and according to the high command, it could be deployed to the border in a fortnight. On the other hand, they expected that the Prussians needed at least seven weeks to mobilize their forces to gain superiority in numbers. There laid a possibility for France to strike first, hopefully enticing Austria, Denmark, and Italy to join in while simultaneously derailing Prussian mobilization. Such an offensive action was expected by the French public, which yearned to "punish" the Prussians for their insolence. However, the French command didn't actually have any fully fleshed out plans. Instead, Napoleon III tried to accommodate both offensive and defensive actions. He split his army into three pieces: I Corps under Marshal Patrice MacMahon in Alsace, VI Corps under Marshal François Canrobert at Châlons, and the Army of the Rhine under his imperial command at Metz. Though named "corps," the first two groupings were actually army-sized.

The naming of those provides a glimpse into the issues plaguing the French high command. The emperor wanted to capitalize on a possible military victory for himself, making his army groupings reminiscent of his uncle's more famous *Grande Armée*. Thus, in a sense, he exiled his most celebrated and capable marshals to field the "smaller" corps, while one of his best commanders, if not his best commander, Marshal Achille Bazaine, was only given provisional command over his army in Metz until Napoleon arrived from Paris. However, Bazaine was under strict orders not to do anything without his permission. Adding insult to injury, members of his imperial headquarters consisted of the freshly promoted Marshal Edmond Leboeuf and Generals Lebrun and Jarras. Together with Napoleon himself, the headquarters had almost no actual military experience. After arriving at Metz on July 28th, the emperor tried to ask Bazaine for assistance in planning an offensive, yet the marshal had no advice to offer. On the other hand, MacMahon tried to show some initiative, asking for some orders on how to proceed in the case of a French assault, but he was ignored. In the end, Leboeuf and Lebrun chose a defensive course of action, massing the Army of the Rhine in Lorraine and waiting for the Prussians.

However, the cracks in the leadership were only the tip of Napoleon's troubles. By late July, only about two-thirds of the planned forces were deployed on the front line. The railways were congested, and troops arrived in smaller, often disjointed groups, commonly without their primary armaments. This meant that units needed to be assembled and armed after arriving, which led to some soldiers not being battle-ready upon arrival at the border.

Furthermore, eagerness for the war quickly dissipated, both among the troops and common citizens. This forced Napoleon to leave about fifteen thousand valuable troops in Paris to secure his reign while he was on the front. Realizing that the regular 400,000 to 500,000 troops the high command counted on most likely wouldn't be enough, a call for volunteers was issued. In a nation with a population of about thirty-five million, only four thousand enlisted, showing how little the French actually cared for the war by then. All the while, soldier morale and discipline were at a horrendous low point. Many were dropping parts of their equipment, while whole units would just wander off to a nearby village or town, looking for some entertainment. Common recruits simply ignored their officers whenever they felt like it.

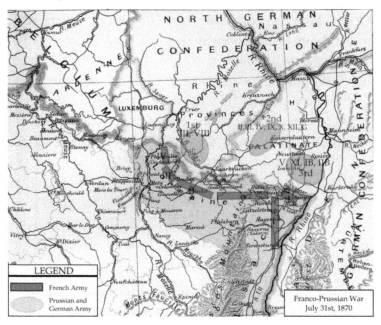

A map depicting the initial positions of both the French and the Prussian forces. Source: https://commons.wikimedia.org

Moreover, they often questioned their orders and instructions, which went all the way up to the emperor himself. They doubted even the larger strategic picture, despite often having no grasp of the tactics. Overall, this proved to be a personal blow to Napoleon, whose regime was supposed to be a military one, one that was secured by a loyal army. France's position in the war seemed to worsen by the day, despite the projections for an early advantage. In contrast, the Germans only gained strength as mobilization went on.

Initially, the proclamation of war caught Moltke and his General Staff off guard. Many Prussian officers were given leave just a few days prior; thus, he had to scramble to recall them all. Nevertheless, the Prussian military practiced mobilization during peacetime, and it quickly started rolling out. Officers planned railway routes and the transportation of their units, sending them to designated grouping areas. Thanks to their much better railroad system, Prussians had about five times as many trains running daily compared to the French. All of that made Prussian mobilization an organized event rather than the ad hoc mess of their opponents, even though it wasn't a fully expected war. It is interesting to mention that another organizational improvement the Prussian military made just prior to the war was the introduction of modern metal dog tags; it was the first modern army in the world to do so. Though this improvement did little to help functionality and mobilization, as it served only as an identification tool for fallen soldiers, it does showcase how well prepared the Prussian Army had become.

In the years prior to the war, Moltke toured down the front lines, inspecting the expected concentration areas and ironing out any inefficiencies and liabilities. He was aware that mobilization was never a simple affair, no matter how well thought out it was. This was especially true for the Prussians' south Germanic allies. There were some accounts of their trains being overcrowded, units getting sunburnt during their marches toward the front, and drunken disobedience, caused by soldiers drinking alcohol instead of water. It is likely similar pictures could've been seen among the Prussian troops but to a much lesser extent. Regardless, the overall German discipline was much higher than among the French.

The Prussian home front was also in much better spirits than the French, with many enlisting on their own. According to some contemporaries, almost all able-bodied men between twenty and thirty-eight years of age were conscripted. Although this is clearly an exaggeration, it paints a picture of Prussian morale and the functionality of its military conscription system. However, a substantial number of volunteers were young university students whose fitness and training were subpar. They simply didn't have enough time to prepare under the Prussian service system. Nevertheless, they compensated for those failings with their enthusiasm. Combining that general fighting spirit with a well-organized mobilization system allowed the Prussian forces to gather 320,000 battle-ready troops by the early days of August. They caught up with French numerical superiority much quicker than most expected.

While the troops amassed, Moltke initially positioned his troops behind the Rhine, Saar, and Moselle Rivers, using them as a natural barrier if the French attacked first. While they amassed, he divided his forces into three armies. The First Army was under the command of General Karl von Steinmetz, and it was located in the northernmost sector of the front line, between Trier and Saarlouis. In the center was the Second Army, commanded by the king's nephew, Prince Friedrich Karl. It was located near Saarbrücken, and it represented the largest of the Prussian forces. Crown Prince Friedrich Wilhelm, the heir to the Prussian throne, was given control of the Third Army, which was positioned around Karlsruhe in the south. As it was to be expected, this southernmost force mostly consisted of the southern Germanic allies—Bavaria, Baden, and Württemberg. Moltke remained skeptical about them joining in the war until the very end and thus refused to supply their junior officers with the same detailed maps Prussians used. It is also worth noting that these troops were caught in the middle of rearming with the newer breechloading rifle.

Finally, unlike Napoleon and his indecisive staff, Moltke and the *Generalstab* were more than prepared to utilize their troops to the best of their extent. In case the French concentrated their troops in the south, either defensively or to attack Baden, the First and Second Armies would push into France, swinging to the southwest to flank. In contrast, if Napoleon decided to keep his troops at Metz or even try to invade the Rhineland, the Third Army would maneuver into the French rear, cutting off communications with Paris and flanking the Army of the Rhine. During the last days of July, the French Army began preparations to do exactly that. Napoleon and his command began to feel public pressure to do something, and even General Charles Frossard, one of his favorite officers, had advocated for days that they attack the border town of Saarbrücken. On July 29th, 1870, the emperor authorized the attack, and the French soldiers began positioning for an advance into Germany.

However, this attack proved to be more of a publicity stunt for the emperor. His troops attacked on August 2nd, encountering only sporadic resistance by the Prussians, mostly skirmishing with their patrols. In those small-scale conflicts, their Chassepot proved its superiority, for the German forces usually scattered. As the French divisions approached Saarbrücken, the single Prussian division defending it more or less withdrew, so no major combat took place. Upon taking hold of the town, Napoleon and Frossard immediately hailed it as a grand victory, something even the belligerent French public had a hard time believing. Such pompousness was quickly debunked since the French Army withdrew almost as quickly as it invaded after realizing that the Prussians were finalizing their initial mobilization and moving their troops across the Rhine toward them.

Overall, the brief invasion of Saarbrücken was not only an exercise in futility but also a serious blunder. Firstly, it further deteriorated the relations between Marshal Bazaine and Napoleon III. Bazaine, who had more experience and a higher rank than

Frossard, was relegated to a supporting position. Bazaine himself knew that there was no point to this attack unless the French Army was to push hard and deep into Prussia, which was unreal. Despite that, he tried to organize a proper enveloping advance onto Saarbrücken, but he was plainly ignored. From then on, Marshal Bazaine became more obstructive than cooperative. Even worse was the fact that this half-measured attack proved that the emperor had no military talent, ordering troops that were a linking pin between the Army of the Rhine and MacMahon's I Corps farther south to join in the attack on Saarbrücken. Without thinking it through, Napoleon and Leboeuf basically left MacMahon without the proper support he would dearly need in the upcoming days.

Marshal Bazaine (top) and Marshal MacMahon (bottom). Source:
https://commons.wikimedia.org

Such a miscalculation could also be partially attributed to French intelligence. While the Prussian cavalry constantly roamed the border regions, French reconnaissance was sporadic and shoddy. Most information coming to Napoleon and his headquarters came from newspapers and foreign war correspondents, which were aided by their own conjectures. When the French ordered the attack on Saarbrücken, it's likely they had little clue that the Prussians were only a few days away from being ready for an invasion of their own. Seeing that the French were basically holding their lines at Metz, disregarding the tactically irrelevant advance on Saarbrücken, Moltke decided to swing the Third Army into MacMahon's I Corps, driving into the Vosges mountain range, before swinging to the north and forcing the French into a pocket. It was a calculated risk on his part, as it would essentially cut off Crown Prince Friedrich Wilhelm's Third Army from the rest of the Prussian forces for several days. Yet, Moltke had all the confidence in the crown prince and his numerical superiority of 125,000 Germans against MacMahon's 45,000 French soldiers.

The French high command, for the most part, was unaware of exact German movements but got wind of it from captured Prussian soldiers and a local chief of police who noticed the enemy approaching. It was these scraps of intelligence that forced the French to retreat from Saarbrücken to their original defensive positions by August 5th, yet by then, MacMahon's corps was under attack. The Prussian Third Army made its initial engagement a day before, attacking a single French division defending Wissembourg. It was an 18th-century defensive fort that overlooked an important junction for Bavaria, Strasbourg, and Lower Alsace. However, in the years prior to the war, that fortification lost its funding, and its state was far from ideal. Further adding to MacMahon's trouble was the fact that he had only four divisions in total, spread to cover the entire southern French flank across the Vosges, making his lines too thinly spread. This meant that it was unlikely he had enough time to react and reposition his men in the case of a Prussian advance.

By the early morning of August 4th, the French cavalry finally made contact with the advancing German troops. A local official had noticed the German movements and alarmed the local French authorities the day before. However, it was dismissed as an insignificant border clash. While the Wissembourg command was reporting it as such, the Prussian artillery began its bombardment. Initially, the French seemed to have an advantage. Using their fortified positions and superior firepower of the Chassepot and the mitrailleuse, they pummeled the Bavarian soldiers who crossed the Lauter River that ran in front of the fort. The mitrailleuse filled the attacking soldiers with special dread, as it often tore bodies into shreds. The French artillery also managed to have an initial impact, showering the advancing troops with their shells. Nonetheless, the French quickly lost their advantage. The Prussian command was aware they had only a single division, one that was tightly packed in the town and its fortification. This made their usual enveloping tactics work almost perfectly as they began spreading out, surrounding the defensive forces. Soon, a few of the Prussian artillery guns also crossed the river, providing a more accurate supportive fire and limiting how effectively the French garrison could fire at the advancing forces.

As the town itself became engulfed in door-to-door combat, its inhabitants, led by their mayor, began pleading with the French soldiers to retreat and to spare their homes from what they saw as a futile resistance. Parts of the French troops were routed, an act likely facilitated by the fact that their commanding officer was killed early in the day from artillery bombardment shrapnel. Other French troops, especially those that were encircled in the town, had no other option than to fight. They chose to make a stoic stand. However, in the end, they were overrun, and by the afternoon, Wissembourg was in German hands. Despite that, the casualties were similar on both sides, with about 1,500 men killed and wounded, though several hundred more Frenchmen were captured.

An illustration from 1899 depicting the close combat at Wissembourg.
Source: https://commons.wikimedia.org

After the battle, the Prussian commanders realized two important things. One was that the French tactic of grouping their entire divisions in an effort to maximize their firepower was wrong, though intuitive. The Chassepot was indeed a much better rifle, both in precision and range, but by condensing their soldiers in one spot, the French were just making it easier for the Prussians to pummel them with their superior artillery, breaking both their spirits and defenses while flanking them surprisingly easy. The second lesson was that their Bavarian allies were only slightly better soldiers than the French. They lacked discipline, especially when under fire. Without the training the Prussians went through, their allies fired too quickly and without proper aim, ignoring direct orders and looking for any reason to break the fire line. Furthermore, after the battle was done, the Bavarians led the looting, searching for food and drink. The Prussians' discipline would be hammered into them in the following weeks.

As the German Third Army was advancing in the south, Moltke began to orchestrate his overarching plan of forcing the French Army into a cauldron. He planned to strike at the heart of Napoleon's forces with the strong Second Army, with the principal target being Frossard's new positions at Spicheren and Forbach, an important supply depot for the French. By attacking at the center and aiming at such an important target, Moltke hoped to suck in the rest of the French troops while the First Army moved up from the north and the Third Army from the south. It was a reasonable plan, despite the fact that the Third Army still hadn't moved through the Vosges yet. However, Moltke's grand design was almost ruined by General Steinmetz. Despite being a grizzled veteran, in 1870, he was far past his prime. Some of his peers even claimed he was slipping into senility. Nevertheless, he was the people's hero and a close friend to King Wilhelm, assuring his commanding position. Having such a strong position in the Prussian Army, Steinmetz decided to take matters into his own hands and ignored Moltke's orders. Instead of taking his forces, the smallest of the three German armies, across the Saar River on the Second Army's right flank to feel out the French positions there, he swiped south toward Frossard.

This proved to be a critical error. With such an irrational movement, Steinmetz cut off the advance of the Second Army under Prince Friedrich Karl, who methodically followed Moltke's plan. Thus, it was the First Army that engaged the center of the French forces, though not on Steinmetz's direct orders. One of his divisional generals reached Spicheren on August 6th and thought the French were retreating. Thus, he ordered a full-on attack on what was supposed to be the French rearguard. Yet, in reality, General Frossard dug in the superior positions around it, using the hilly terrain to his advantage, and he had no plans to yield. Moltke's plan was on the brink of destruction at that moment, as the French held far superior positions while the Prussian attack was made without any regard to grand strategic development. And all because of the overzealousness of Steinmetz and his subordinate officer.

Beyond the initial miscalculation of the French forces, Steinmetz's division general made another mistake. He attacked without having all his troops with him, sending just a couple of battalions, which arrived first. When initial contact was made, the strength of French fire signaled that it wasn't merely a rearguard. The Prussian forces came close to the French positions but were stopped in their tracks by the French guns. For a while, the German artillery was able to keep the French forces at bay, but by the afternoon, the Prussian troops took too many casualties and began retreating. Frossard then allowed for a formidable counterattack, which managed to push back both the retreating German forces as well as the troops that were just arriving on the battlefield. Had he unleashed the full potential of the French forces, he might have dealt a painful defeat to the Prussians. Yet, he clung to the defensive strategy, refusing to leave the safety of his fortified high ground. That gave enough time for the Prussians to regroup.

Soon, Prince Friedrich Karl's units began to arrive, immediately shifting to fighting formations without waiting for the direct command to do so. More importantly, Steinmetz's division general was relieved of command, giving the reins to the more competent General Constantin von Alvensleben. The Prussians then began to amass their troops and once again increased pressure on the French, slowly pushing them back while simultaneously fanning out to begin proper encirclement. Frossard's men continued to rain shells on the attackers, but here, the proper Prussian discipline, stubbornness, and numerical superiority began to shine through. They continued to advance relentlessly, maintaining their skirmish lines despite casualties. All the while, the Prussian artillery not only grew in size but also found more favorable positions, increasing their pressure on the French defenses. By the late afternoon, Alvensleben had gathered enough of his own troops as reserves to thrust them at the French flanks. Combined with artillery fire, this proved enough to dislodge the French from Spicheren. By the evening, Frossard ordered a full retreat back to the defensive line on the Moselle River.

An 1890 drawing of Prussian troops advancing at Spicheren. Source: https://commons.wikimedia.org

Thus, Spicheren was nearly a disaster for the Prussians. It was avoided more by French blunders than anything else. Had Frossard unleashed a proper counterattack, the Germans would have most likely shattered. Furthermore, the battle lasted long enough for him to receive reinforcements, but the faulty relations and communication between French commanders led to disaster. Frossard initially asked for just two brigades, but Bazaine refused to send them. His lines were already thin, he said, while at the time, Frossard was still unsure if the Prussian attack was a serious one. The animosity between the two officers only dulled Bazaine's willingness to aid his compatriot. However, had Frossard asked properly and timely for reinforcements, Bazaine surely wouldn't have let him down. Yet, in the early afternoon, Frossard messaged him, saying that he believed he would be victorious, mistaking the Prussian respite for defeat. Only a couple of hours later, he sent a telegram stating he had been outflanked and on the verge of defeat. By then, it was too late, as Bazaine's troops needed several hours to arrive. In fact, Bazaine sent a full division to Frossard, but they managed to arrive only as his soldiers were retreating.

In the end, the Battle of Spicheren exemplified significant characteristics on both sides. For better or worse, the Prussian officers showed more proactivity and acted upon their own instincts, while the French were reined in by their orders. The latter were also constricted by their overly defensive strategy, while the Prussians showed their tenacity and stubbornness to push through the mud and grit. It also showcased the swarming feature of the Prussian advance. They often made contact with the French with a limited number of troops, testing out their defenses while slowly amassing their troops for an attack if the opportunity seemed right. This made it rather hard for the French commanders to determine if the clash was a mere skirmish or a full-blown attack. By the time they figured it out, it usually proved too late. Spicheren also showed how deadly the battles could be, as both sides suffered substantial losses. The Prussians casualties were just below five thousand out of a force of about thirty-seven thousand, while the French were around four thousand of a total twenty-nine thousand soldiers. Nevertheless, these were merely initial clashes and were still limited in scope.

Chapter 5 – Spreading the Flames of War: The Prussian Invasion

The victories of Wissembourg and Spicheren were only the opening scenes in what was soon to become a French tragedy. As the German First and Second Armies were only springing into action, the Third Army, under Crown Prince Friedrich Wilhelm, began to push deeper into French territory.

He planned to deal with MacMahon on the eastern slopes of the Vosges, securing his rear, before swiveling north to aid the main Prussian attack. After Wissembourg, his troops lost contact with the retreating French troops; thus, on August 5th, the German cavalry spread around the region, searching for the enemy. Friedrich Wilhelm thought MacMahon retreated to the safety of the fortress in Strasbourg, farther to the south. Instead, his scouts found the French I Corps entrenched at Froeschwiller-Woerth, a group of villages in the Vosges only twelve miles (twenty kilometers) southeast of Wissembourg. Such a decision was backed both strategically and tactically. Firstly, Froeschwiller was an important railroad junction. If the Prussians seized it, it would isolate the forces in Strasbourg while easing German resupplying. In tactical terms, it was one of *positions magnifique*, as the French called them, a location that was easily defendable. The four villages compromising the Froeschwiller-Woerth basin were linked by a lateral road, so it was easily enforceable. They held the high ground while also forming a semicircular line with the Sauer River beneath them. Most positions had clear fields of fire in all directions, while the hill slopes were dotted with vine and hop plantations, making advancing through them a nightmare for the attackers. Indeed, the Froeschwiller-Woerth was a position that could make the most out of the Chassepot and the mitrailleuse.

Nevertheless, the Froeschwiller-Woerth basin had one major defensive flaw. It was exposed to flanking and encirclement, especially if no other troops were near enough to support its defense. All that the Prussians needed to achieve a victory was sufficient numerical superiority, which they had. The Third Army that marched toward Froeschwiller-Woerth numbered almost 100,000 men, while there were only 50,000 French defenders. Despite that, MacMahon still planned his counterattack. In the early hours of August 6th, he ordered the nearby V Corps, which was thirty thousand men strong under General Pierre de Failly, to be prepared for either attacking the Prussian flank as they moved through the Vosges or even encirclement if the enemy proved inactive. Regardless of MacMahon's wishful thinking, Crown Prince Friedrich Wilhelm was diligent and planned to use his numerical advantage to flank and surround the French forces. Furthermore, he planned to do it properly, gathering his army and attacking the fortified positions in an organized manner. Yet, like at Spicheren, one of the middle-ranked officers hotheadedly committed to an early attack.

As forward units of several Third Army corps unexpectedly stumbled upon the French positions, their commanding officer ordered his men to attack immediately, without waiting for the rest of the Third Army. Thus, the Battle of Froeschwiller-Woerth began on August 6th instead of on August 7th as the crown prince had planned. To make matters worse, they faced the French left wing, which was held by numerous battle-hardened veterans who served in Crimea, Algeria, and Italy. As the gunfire began to echo, the arriving Prussian troops immediately began deploying into battle lines, expanding the existing German front line. Friedrich Wilhelm was furious and tried to delay the battle, sending messengers to the forward lines, but it was too late. Froeschwiller-Woerth was turning into an another Spicheren.

The initial clashes at Froeschwiller-Woerth were eerily similar to the battle that raged at roughly the same time near Spicheren. The first attacks, carried out by mixed Prussian, Bavarian, and Baden-Württembergian troops, thinned their advancing columns into skirmish lines, slowly enfolding the French positions. Yet, their advance was almost nonexistent, as the defenders picked them off with their superior rifles and the mitrailleuse, which were further supported by their artillery. The marshy and hilly battleground only further bogged down the German advance, while the surrounding woods provided little cover against the French cannons. Even the best trained Prussian soldiers stood little chance as the defenders rained down upon them with hot lead. The German casualties piled up, and some of the troops even lost their nerve and ran away from combat, most notably the Bavarians. As the day approached noon, the battle was slipping away from the Germans, and if the French had mounted a timely counterattack, the Germans could have faltered. Yet, once again, the French command decided to remain on the defense.

Trying to salvage the battle, Friedrich Wilhelm sent two of his adjutants to rein in and organize the assault, as the crown prince was literally stuck in traffic traveling to Froeschwiller-Woerth. Upon their arrival, his adjutants found some friction between the Prussians and the Bavarians. The latter felt they were being sacrificed to save

Prussian lives, despite all of them dying along the front line. Some of the Bavarian officers even refused to commit their troops to an attack, agreeing to do so only under direct pressure from the crown prince. Nevertheless, the Third Army corps continued to roll in, expanding their flanks and slowly encircling MacMahon. More importantly, the German artillery began arriving in greater numbers and started pummeling French defensive positions. As the battle dragged on, the artillery fire began to suppress the defenders, simultaneously countering the French cannons, destroying their mitrailleuse nests, and demoralizing the troops. The significance of the Prussian artillery is illustrated by the French commanders who claimed that without it, they would have easily defended against any German assault.

Karte zur Schlacht bei Wörth (6. Aug. 1870).

"THE BATTERIES PASSED THROUGH THE STREETS ENCUMBERED WITH TROOPS OF THE

*A battle position at Froeschwiller-Woerth depicting Prussian cauldron tactics
(top) and the Prussian artillery moving through the streets of Woerth
(bottom). Source: https://commons.wikimedia.org*

By the early afternoon, the Third Army was deployed almost in its full strength. The envelopment was finalizing, leaving MacMahon with a single option to restore his battle fortunes. He ordered his heavy cavalry reserves to charge at the advancing Prussian flanks; in other words, it was a last resort, "Hail Mary" attempt. The counterattack quickly turned into a disaster, as the Prussian rapid-firing guns proved the era of cavalry charges was gone. None of the French horsemen managed to get near the German lines. With that, the battle was pretty much resolved. The Prussians' relentless advance and artillery fire began to wear down the French, especially on their right flank, which lacked experience, being compromised mostly of freshly recruited troops. They crumbled and fled, leaving flanks and the rear of the rest of MacMahon's corps exposed, which the German troops immediately used to their advantage. Additionally, the Prussian troops and artillery harassed the retreating French troops. Soon, the French left wing began to falter, while the German troops managed to advance even on the heavily defended center. One by one, the French divisions fell into disarray, retreating in mass panic. There were some valiant exceptions among the French, but they were easily silenced by the swarming Prussian troops. By late afternoon, it was clear the battle was won by the Third Army.

As night fell, darkness covered up the scattering of what remained of MacMahon's I Corps, preventing even more devastating results. The end tally for the French was about twenty thousand; about half were wounded and killed, while the rest were captured. It represents a loss of about 40 percent of the I Corps. On the German side, the losses were around ten thousand, or just 10 percent of the Third Army's strength. With losses in men as well as in equipment, the French I Corps was knocked out of the war for a while, allowing the crown prince to choose if he wanted to pursue them or close on the Army of the Rhine at Metz. With the victory at Froeschwiller-Woerth, the Germans showed the French and the rest of the world that their invasion, unlike the initial French theatrics near Saarbrücken, was a serious undertaking.

It should be noted that at Froeschwiller-Woerth, apart from their loose and opportunistic tactics, the Germans exhibited their less-than-civilized face. Despite this war being a struggle between two nations, the two armies also had some non-national troops. On the Prussian side, those were Poles, while the French had their Algerian Berber troops. At one point during the battle, the latter were exhibiting stiff resistance, despite being surrounded. The Algerian regiment fought on, causing frustration to the attackers. The Prussians and Bavarians began claiming that the Berbers were committing various atrocities, mutilating and killing the wounded Germans, despite not really being in a position to do so. Thus, they began their revenge, hunting them down and executing every wounded Algerian they found. Such monstrous behavior was only eased by the fact that the Berbers were seen as beast-like dark-skinned barbarians. Even Bismarck later approved of such actions, claiming that Algerians, or as he called them "black men," "are beasts of prey, and ought to be shot down."

Regardless of such vile outbursts, the Germans continued their advance through France. For days, they were met without any serious opposition as their troops plundered and looted the French countryside, looking for supplies they needed. As they slowly enclosed around the main body of the French Army, France was slowly dissolving into internal turmoil. In Paris, the military violently suppressed outbursts of disappointment when Ollivier was replaced. The new prime minister was General Charles Cousin de Montauban, who was much more on the extreme right side of the political spectrum and a person much closer to Napoleon III. Regardless, Paris was slowly descending into a revolutionary atmosphere similar to 1789 and 1848. The emperor was losing public support, while defeatism began to corrode the French masses, though their national zeal kept some of the fighting spirit alive.

The losses at Spicheren and Froeschwiller-Woerth caused ripples in the French military organization and hierarchy as well. Napoleon reluctantly and gradually relinquished control over the Army of the Rhine to Marshal Bazaine. It was only on August 11th, when the legislative body in Paris tried to impeach Leboeuf, that the emperor realized he had to hand over command to Bazaine regardless of their personal rivalries. Yet, Napoleon still dragged this on as long as he could, even forcing Bazaine to take in members of Leboeuf's cabinet into his staff. It was only on August 14th that Bazaine finally was given full control of the main body of the French Army, although the emperor still tried to influence the marshal's decisions, playing on his official title of commander-in-chief. As Napoleon and Bazaine were playing this tug-of-war, the French troops stood still, doing nothing and losing vital time for any maneuvers. They remained centered around Metz. All the while, Moltke's three armies were gradually enveloping them. By August 14th, his cavalry units were already biting into the communication lines between Metz and Paris.

It is only around this time that the first French units began moving away from Metz; however, this was both too late and too leisurely. The main problem facing the French defenders was the fact that Metz lay on the eastern banks of the Moselle River, which was open to Prussian attacks. On August 13th, Napoleon issued Bazaine an order to retreat westward to Verdun, falling as far back as Châlons. He refused, claiming that retreating at that moment was unfavorable since the Germans were arriving. By that time, the Third Army was closing in from the south, taking control of Nancy, a junction in the principal supply line for the Prussians. More surprisingly, the French allowed that without a fight. By doing so, Bazaine's only line of retreat was, in fact, via Verdun. Yet, by August 14th, the German First Army clashed with Bazaine's rearguard of the

Army of the Rhine. A short and rather half-hearted battle took place at Borny, on the outskirts of Metz.

This conflict was instigated by middle-ranked Prussian officers, but this time, Steinmetz reined in his troops. He didn't want to commit to the attack, fearing more reprimands from Moltke and King Wilhelm. In the end, the Germans lost about 5,000 of their soldiers, while the French fared better with only 3,600 casualties. Neither side was willing to turn this into a more serious battle. On the one hand, Moltke was rightfully afraid the French were planning some kind of counterattack while his forces were still only arriving. On the other side, Bazaine ignored Leboeuf's warnings from the days after the battles at Spicheren and Froeschwiller-Woerth that the French commanders had to shift into a counteroffensive when the Germans first showed signs of faltering. Once again, had they done something more than staying put, the French may have thrown a wrench into Moltke's plan. Instead, Bazaine remained inactive, even stopping any further retreats. It seemed like he lost the will to fight, almost as if it was out of spite toward Napoleon.

Having wasted more than a week on personal squabbles and day-to-day insignificances, such as the cutlery supply of his cantinas, Bazaine was finally on the move. On August 15th, the marshal finally started his retreat, transporting his remaining troops over to the western banks of the Moselle. Even then, his action was sluggish, as he paused the retreat in the early hours of the 16th to deal with the confusion created by the withdrawal. All the while, the French retreat was under constant harassment by the Prussian cavalry, meaning that the wounded troops and supply transports needed armed escorts, which only added to the difficulties of evacuating from Metz. Luckily for Bazaine, the Prussians were not yet fully in striking distance, as only parts of the Second Army were near enough. In fact, on August 15th, Moltke was enacting a pivoting maneuver centered around several corps of the First and Second Army near Metz while crossing the Moselle with his flanks. It was somewhat of a calculated risk, as at that moment, the entire Prussian invasion was susceptible to a French counteroffensive. Nevertheless, the Prussian *Generalstab* saw little incentive among the French for such actions and decided to gamble.

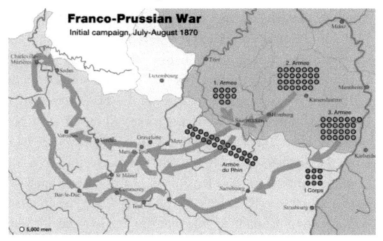

A map showing the movements and important places from the early stages of the Franco-Prussian War. Source: https://www.quora.com

On August 16th, the retreating French forces came into the firing range of the Prussian artillery, further scaring Bazaine. He thought that Moltke was trying to cut him off from Metz, which still had its garrison and formidable fortified defenses, as well as trying to encircle him on the open field. Thus, instead of continuing his retreat, he entrenched himself at Gravelotte, keeping an open road to Metz. That was exactly what Moltke wanted, as he sought to prevent the French from establishing a new defensive line at Châlons, which would put both the Meuse and the Marne Rivers between the two forces. Furthermore, Châlons was the place where the remains of MacMahon's troops and a French reserve army were gathering. Despite that, Moltke still didn't plan a serious confrontation with the French, as the Prussian troops were still gathering and positioning around Metz and the Moselle.

Regardless of Moltke's plans, the freedom of action exhibited by middle-ranking officers once again drew the Prussians into an unwanted battle. In the early morning of August 16th, commander of the Prussian III Corps ordered an attack on the French positions alongside the road to Verdun, despite being warned that the enemy had massed considerable troops there. A Prussian commander thought these were mere rearguards of the retreating French Army and wanted to separate it from the presumed main bulk farther west. He ordered his two divisions to take Mars-la-Tour, a village alongside the road. Unwittingly, he engaged four French corps, with the added trouble of having no nearby reinforcements available to him for hours. The French, on the other hand, had the entire Army of the Rhine nearby. Thus, the Battle of Mars-la-Tour should have been an easy victory for the French.

The start of the skirmish certainly signaled as much, as the French quickly drove off the Prussian attack. The Prussian division was smashed by French superior numbers and rifles. The initial breakdown was only avoided by the Prussian artilleries' suppressing fire, which stopped the French from exploiting their early advantage. As midday closed in, the French were in a perfect position to wipe out the entire III Corps, even exploiting the situation for a much serious counteroffensive, as the Prussian forces were divided and vulnerable. The French corps generals were indecisive, waiting for an order from Bazaine. Among them was the recently demoted Leboeuf, who now urged the marshal not to squander their advantage. Yet, Bazaine forbade them from acting. He was only concerned with maintaining an open road back to Metz. Nevertheless, by the early afternoon, the single Prussian corps remained under heavy fire, taking massive casualties. In a desperate act, the Prussian commander ordered his cavalry on a suicide flanking attack to relieve some pressure from the infantry. Despite delaying the order for a while, the Prussian cavalry finally attacked. By utilizing the hilly terrain, they managed to surprise part of the French artillery line, disrupting and panicking them. More than half of them died, yet the horsemen managed to buy the rest of the III Corps some time.

This act only reinforced Bazaine's defensive disposition, going as far as to personally ride to Leboeuf and stopping his independent action of cutting off the Prussian line of retreat. Instead, the marshal ordered him to retreat to Gravelotte. As the afternoon dragged on, the Prussian artillery batteries exhibited their independence, amassing behind the III Corps on their own. Their potent fire kept the French at bay long enough for the Prussian X Corps to arrive and support their exhausted comrades. During the late afternoon, some local counterattacks were attempted by the French, but they proved futile, as, by then, the Prussian artillery was massed enough to rip them apart. As dusk fell, the battle began to settle into a stalemate. In the early evening, as night was falling, the Prussians tried one last attack, and for a while, chaos expanded throughout the battleground, yet with the cover of darkness, the hostilities fizzled out.

A painting of the Prussian cavalry charge at Mars-la-Tour. Source: https://commons.wikimedia.org

Tactically speaking, the Battle of Mars-la-Tour was a draw, as both sides had similar losses, around sixteen thousand men each. Yet, strategically, it was another loss for the French. Under concealment of night, they withdrew to Gravelotte, yielding the road to Verdun to the Prussians. The Army of the Rhine was slowly being cut off from its retreat lines. Furthermore, despite losing the same number of troops, the Prussians were able to brush them off because of their numerical superiority. Only adding to the inconspicuous disaster was the fact that Bazaine had all the prospects for an easy win. The French could have struck a serious blow to Prince Friedrich Karl and the Second Army, all with the strategic possibility of retreating to Verdun and further stretch the Prussian forces that still had to deal with Metz and its garrison. On an even grander scale, Mars-la-Tour proved to be politically decisive. Any chance of Austria, Italy, or Denmark joining France in the war was now gone. No one would join a war effort that seemed destined to fail.

The next day, Marshal Bazaine shocked his subordinates by ordering a retreat to Plappeville, one of Metz's outlying fortifications. He argued that the withdrawal toward Verdun was too dangerous at the moment, yet most of his generals claimed there was ample possibility to slip away, if not to Verdun then to the northwest and Sedan. Regardless, Bazaine chose Metz, redeploying by the late afternoon to a ridge above Gravelotte, blocking the western approach to the city. Simultaneously, Moltke and Friedrich Karl moved their troops in a swinging motion, cutting off the line between Verdun and Metz and finalizing their encirclement of the French Army. The prince sent numerous patrols, making sure that were no French fighting forces behind their back. To his relief, he found only stragglers and deserters. With that, the battle lines finally shifted 180 degrees. Initially, the French fought on the west and the Germans on the east side of the front, while at Mars-la-Tour, the former fought on the north and the latter on the south. After August 17th, the Prussians' backs were turned west, toward Paris, while the French had their backs turned east, toward Metz and ultimately Berlin. Regardless, Moltke decided to make his decisive action properly organized, and he reined in his commanders, including Steinmetz, massing his troops in encircling lines.

At the same time, Napoleon III arrived at Châlons, where he met with MacMahon and what was dubbed the Army of Châlons. Upon talking with Marshal MacMahon and the few officers that were present, they agreed that this army should take defensive positions around Paris, hoping to make the Prussian siege of the capital as painful as possible. Yet, the empress and the government in Paris persuaded the weak-willed Napoleon to change his mind, almost ordering him to utilize the last available French fighters for a diversion that would relieve some pressure off Bazaine and the Army of the Rhine. That decision was yet another nail in the coffin. While Napoleon sank deeper into depression, Bismarck visited the front line. He was exalted that the Prussian forces were winning and setting the pace of the war, but he felt slightly appalled by the general's brutality. They were too willing to sacrifice their own men, including Bismarck's son, Herbert, who was wounded in the cavalry charge at Mars-la-Tour. Such brutality would shine through the very next day when the Germans finally attacked Bazaine.

Unlike previous *positions magnifique*, Gravelotte wasn't as strong. The left wing could utilize hills, ravines, and the Moselle to anchor the French defense. In contrast, the French right wing lacked any natural obstacles. That weakness could've been offset by adding additional artillery and troops, something Bazaine ignored. Making his position worse, the marshal put his weakest corps there while positioning his reserves hours away from that vulnerable spot. The battle began on the morning of August 18th, when Prince Friedrich Karl ordered his units to advance. Moltke was determined to utilize more finesse than in previous battles, which was possible this time around, as this clash was anticipated and planned for by both sides. It was also the largest battle of the war, with about 200,000 German soldiers fighting against about 160,000 French troops, with hundreds of cannons on both sides. Despite that, Friedrich Karl initially thought that the forces in the French center were merely a rearguard, so he suspected that Bazaine was retreating to Metz. Thus, he ordered the bulk of the Second Army to engage in a frontal attack. Luckily, Moltke was present at the battlefield and realized the prince's error. He ordered the assault to spread out, sending additional corps to his left wing to help envelop the weak French right wing.

While the Prussian troops were still repositioning, a single division at the center made the first unauthorized attack at the center. They struck at heavily fortified French positions and quickly began to falter. At that crucial moment, General Steinmetz once again disobeyed Moltke. Instead of cutting off the assault, he ordered additional corps to it, taking command of units that were assigned to the Second Army and overreaching his authority. The attack quickly turned into yet another unnecessary slaughter of Prussian soldiers, especially as the flanking corps still weren't ready to attack. Steinmetz sent wave after wave of men, none of whom made any progress. King Wilhelm, who was present at the battlefield, was displeased by the number of his soldiers fleeing the assault, calling them cowards. This only further angered Moltke, who saw that the entire attack was a wasteful massacre of Prussian troops, all of whom he deemed heroes.

A 1910 painting depicting the Prussian infantry advance at Gravelotte.
Source: https://commons.wikimedia.org

The French once again failed to exploit the initial Prussian mistake. By the early afternoon, the Prussian left wing engaged, making any counterattack impossible. All the while, the German artillery masses shredded through the defenses, tearing down French morale along with Frenchmen. By the late afternoon, the fortunes of battle were turning. The French right wing demanded reinforcements and supplies, both of which Bazaine refused. The Prussian troops made a wide flanking maneuver, yet as the French fire was silenced by the artillery, they assumed the French were driven out. Thus, the Prussian left wing attacked prematurely, without fully completing the flanking maneuver, adding to the number of unnecessary casualties. Their initial push was easily repulsed by the Chassepot. Nevertheless, they soon regrouped and properly flanked the French, whose right wing began to collapse. As night closed in, the left-center of the Army of the Rhine also began to crumble under the pressure.

Throughout the afternoon, the general commanding the reserve units tried to gain permission from Bazaine to reinforce the obviously failing right wing, but he could not obtain it. The marshal simply mumbled about defensive positions without issuing many direct orders. To his subordinates, he seemed genuinely uninterested in a fight. Without committing his reserves, Bazaine wasted thirty thousand of his elite soldiers and more than one hundred guns, all while his positions were cracking. Seeing that development, Steinmetz wanted to strike the final blow himself. Indulged by his old friend, Wilhelm I, he ordered a renewed attack on the center. Once again, this led to a senseless slaughter, as the French mitrailleuses continued to mow them down. Moltke remained silent, unable to challenge his king. With the shroud of night, the French right wing finally collapsed. Something similar happened with Steinmetz's frontal assault. Regardless, the battle was coming to an end.

An 1881 painting depicting French casualties at their defensive positions at Gravelotte. Source: https://commons.wikimedia.org

In a strategic sense, the Battle of Gravelotte was a clear French defeat. The Army of the Rhine was enclosed, now cut off even from retreat toward Sedan. The men could only find shelter at Metz, and they didn't have enough food or ammunition to hold off for a long time. Yet, due to the reckless Prussian command, it wasn't a total defeat. King Wilhelm himself didn't see the battle as much of a victory, as the Prussian Army lost about twenty thousand men, while the French losses were only at twelve thousand, including four thousand captives. Had the battle been under Moltke's undisputed command, the Germans would have likely lost fewer men and would have inflicted a much more decisive defeat. Regardless, it is vital to point out that the victory, no matter how flawed, was won by Prussian maneuvering and its superior artillery, which was responsible for roughly 70 percent of French casualties. With the effective loss of the entire Army of the Rhine, France was teetering toward total defeat in the war.

Chapter 6 – Waving the White Flag: The String of French Defeats

After the Battle of Gravelotte, the Franco-Prussian War transformed into a fox hunt for a while, leaving the conflict void of any larger clashes. While the Prussians were chasing the French, the action of their enemies confused everyone, as they lacked any common sense.

In the days after Gravelotte, Bazaine retreated to Metz with an army of 140,000 strong, including roughly 12,000 wounded. That move was essentially a death trap, as the city was already lacking provisions for its garrison and about seventy thousand citizens. Additional mouths were hard to feed, and even water supplies became an issue. The Moselle wasn't the best source of water, as it was somewhat polluted. The only real chance for survival of the now renamed Army of Metz was a breakthrough. Yet, Bazaine was set in his lethargy, which began to spread among his subordinate officers as well. Two lackluster attempts were made on August 26th and 31st, but the Prussians easily pushed them back. The lack of vigor and will is the only explanation to why a fighting force of about

130,000 French soldiers and hundreds of guns were unable to break through the thinned Prussian siege lines. In fact, on August 31ˢᵗ, the initial clash pitted eight French divisions against a single Prussian division. Utilizing Metz's forts to bog down the Prussian redeployment, a successful breakthrough was more than possible.

French cavalrymen photographed in Metz. Source:
https://commons.wikimedia.org

In that scenario, Bazaine had a multitude of possible actions. His Army of Metz could've retreated to the Vosges and threatened Prussian supply lines, or he could have pushed north to Sedan and unite with MacMahon. Or he could have moved in a direction to threaten the flanks or rears of the advancing Prussian forces. Instead, Bazaine remained passive, certain that his breakthrough attempts would eventually fail. His officers quickly reconciled with such a fate, leaving their soldiers to slowly starve. Two attempted sorties only increased the number of wounded, compounding the issue. The marshal was later accused of treason for the entirety of his actions, possibly because he wished to see the Bonaparte regime fall. Though this remains a possibility or at least a partial reasoning behind some of his actions, the sources hint that his defeatist attitude was the far more plausible culprit. He simply lost his will to fight and spread a similar attitude to his own troops as well.

Communication between Metz and Paris was mostly cut off, leaving MacMahon in the dark. He had hints that Bazaine would try to break out and head toward Sedan; thus, he chose to move his army northward from Châlons. He wanted to remain near Paris to help in its defense, yet the orders from Paris were clear—help Bazaine. Not wishing to tarnish his own reputation by abandoning the Army of Metz, MacMahon complied. The only solace he had was the promotion to *general en chef*, now officially outranking the emperor himself. The promotion came from Paris, where Empress Eugénie became more of a monarch than Napoleon III, who was only sinking further into his depression.

While Bazaine's inactivity played right into Moltke's hand once again, MacMahon's actions were puzzling to him. He was unsure of the *general en chef*'s intentions, fearing they may be some kind of feint to draw out and prolong Prussian movement in a wild goose chase while Paris strengthened its defenses. His keen strategic mind was aware that moving the last French fighting force to Sedan, and even worse, taking the northern route to aid the forces in Metz, was a ludicrous move destined to fail. Yet, after his scouts had encountered no other kind of activity from the French for several days, Moltke decided to gamble and commit to chasing MacMahon.

In the prior days, Moltke reformed his armies. Prince Friedrich Karl was the given overarching command of the siege of Metz, including control over the Second Army. This naturally infuriated Steinmetz, but by mid-September, he was relieved of duty and sent to Prussia to become the governor of Posen (modern Poznan). The besieging force numbered around 150,000 men. However, a large chunk of the Second Army was detached from it and given to Crown Prince Albert of Saxony. This became the Fourth Army or the Army of the Meuse. It had around ninety thousand men and was tasked to move westward toward Verdun. On its left wing was the Third Army, which was still under the command of Friedrich Wilhelm; it numbered about 130,000, and it was moving toward the

Meuse and the Marne Rivers, reaching the latter on August 24th. It is worth noting that by that time, more than 100,000 fresh conscripts arrived from Prussia, replacing their losses and even increasing the German fighting force. Worryingly for France, even more troops were still being formed in Prussia.

The freedom to gather and move such large reinforcements was partially aided by the total failure of the French Navy. It outnumbered the Prussian fleet roughly ten to one, and at the start of the war, there were plans to use it for a naval invasion or at least for disruptive actions along the Prussian coastline. However, French ships constantly lacked coal, and their officers lacked familiarity with the seas there. No German or Danish seamen wanted to aid them with their knowledge. Also, hauling coal from France was exhausting, and the Prussians outfitted their shorelines with formidable Krupp cannons that outranged any French naval gun. Overall, they were unable to do anything to jeopardize the Prussian home front. Additionally, as the crisis on the land expanded, what little marines were available for any naval operations were recalled to serve under MacMahon. By September, the French had ceased all naval operations and returned the ships to their harbor, as even their ill-attempted economic blockade proved inefficient.

Regardless, by August 26th, two German armies began their chase. Moltke's bold decision was also playing in favor of Bismarck's plans and political needs. While prior to Gravelotte, Prussia faced little international pressure, its great victory and France's blunder started to create a commotion. The Italians and Austrians became openly concerned with the future of France, while Britain began to ponder the balance of European power. Even the long neutral Russians began to watch with unease at the development in the west. All of the major powers feared that Prussia might fully dismember France. Their restlessness caused politicians in Berlin to worry about the possibility that some kind of unified action from Britain, Russia, Austria, and Italy might be aimed at restraining Prussia. Thus, Bismarck was aware a quick victory was needed to prevent other powers from interfering. So, the chancellor was more than pleased with the possibility of destroying the remaining French forces in a decisive battle. The only hole in his plans was the possibility of capturing the emperor himself, which would prevent Napoleon from arranging a quick peace the Prussians needed.

The first contacts between the pursuing German forces and MacMahon's troops occurred on August 29th, as a French corps and a Prussian corps collided near Buzancy, some twenty-five miles (forty kilometers) south of Sedan. It was clear the two armies were on a collision course, as Moltke planned to catch the French on the left bank of the Meuse. The initial clash at Buzancy lasted for a while before the French corps retreated north, taking up positions at Beaumont, which was twice as close to Sedan. Early on the next day, the Germans managed to surprise the tired French troops there, routing them rather quickly. The clash was short-lived, leaving the French with a staggering 7,500 casualties, while Germans lost only 3,500 men. The rest of the French Corps scattered farther north to Mouzon, where the main body of MacMahon's army was trying to cross on the left bank of the Meuse.

The skirmish at Beaumont signaled to MacMahon that the Prussians were advancing on him from the south as well from the east. Continuing his river crossing would be suicide. Furthermore, he was cut off both from Metz and Paris, and he could only retreat northward to Sedan, which had an outdated 17th-century fort on the right bank of the Meuse, near the Belgian border. He had two possible options. Either he would attempt a last stand at Sedan or cross into Belgium, knocking his army out of the war as international law stipulated. Without much pondering, he ordered his troops toward the old fort. Moltke was also aware of the situation. Thus, he ordered the Third Army, which was on the left bank of the Meuse, to move directly toward Sedan, while the Army of the Meuse was ordered to encircle the fort from the east and north, effectively cutting off MacMahon from Belgium. With that, the Army of Châlons would be trapped, surrounded by the Germans on all sides.

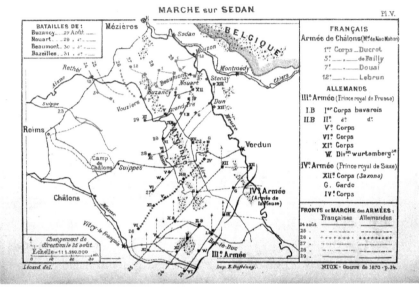

A map depicting Prussians (blue) advancing toward the French (red), forcing them toward Sedan. Source: https://commons.wikimedia.org

Having little time to prepare his positions, MacMahon acted too conservatively, arranging his troops in a tight triangle in front of Sedan. This was erroneous, as the French troops would then be perfectly gathered to be torn to shreds by the Prussian artillery while having nowhere to retreat to apart from Sedan. Furthermore, the outdated fortifications no longer provided sufficient support or defense. Even the Meuse offered little help. The German guns on the left bank of the river could still fire at the French troops massed on the right bank in front of the castle. For Moltke, it was the perfect trap, and even the French generals were aware of that. Moltke just needed a bit of time to finalize his encirclement maneuvers.

However, the battle once again prematurely started by an overzealous middle-ranked officer. In the early hours of September 1ˢᵗ, a single Bavarian corps engaged the southernmost tip of French defenses. Since the rest of the German troops were still not positioned for a fight, the Bavarians were repulsed, and their initial attack seemed to be yet another waste of German lives. Regardless, they were quickly reinforced as the rest of the German units continued to assume their given positions. As they arrived, the artillery batteries began firing upon the French positions, slowly massing and taking favorable positions for a bombardment. In those early hours of the battle, just as it was turning into full-blown combat, MacMahon was seriously wounded. Shrapnel from an artillery shell lacerated his leg, making him unable to command. He made General Auguste Ducrot, a veteran and trusted officer, the commander-in-chief. However, this was almost immediately disputed by the recently appointed General Emmanuel Wimpffen, who held higher seniority over the officers. This led to confusion, as for a while, the French troops weren't sure who held the reins. Eventually, Wimpffen took general command, but disorder persisted.

As the Prussian envelopment continued, their artillery assumed positions on the slopes overlooking the dug-in French troops. It wasn't long before their overlapping fire began to pummel the defenses and the defenders. Both began to crumble under such pressure, for about seven hundred artillery guns rained shells upon them. By noon, the German artillery was capable of shattering every French attempt of counterattack, battery fire, and even the mitrailleuse nest in a matter of minutes. Their fire, precision, and coordination were almost textbook, far beyond what should have been possible in the chaos of battle. Yet, they had superior positions as well as guns, while the French had no way to reach them nor disrupt their fire. Furthermore, by midday, the defenders were more or less left without any support of their own artillery, as it was either destroyed or abandoned. Eventually, the German batteries were able to relocate to different positions, searching for the best angle at a target, with several batteries aiming at a single spot. Thus, shells rained from various overlapping directions, making finding suitable shelter almost impossible for the French.

With such unbearable conditions and with French units slowly disintegrating, both Wimpffen and Ducrot realized they needed a breakthrough. They organized two almost simultaneous attempts, one toward the west and one toward the southeast. These attempts weren't coordinated or properly organized, so they failed miserably. The Prussian artillery broke them easily, leaving infantrymen to finish off the French. All the while, the French units continued to dissolve, with chaotic masses of soldiers trying to seek refuge inside the fort. All the cracks and gaps left by them were quickly filled with the German units, which exploited every opportunity to the fullest.

As the afternoon dragged on, the French forces were nearing total collapse. They had about seventeen thousand casualties, with another twenty-one thousand taken as prisoners. The Germans had lost nine thousand men altogether. Seeing that there was no real way out, Napoleon III conferred with his generals. All but Wimpffen were in favor of surrender, and the emperor complied. A white flag was erected on the walls of Sedan, while Napoleon's adjutant rode under one toward the Prussian headquarters. He was carrying a letter of surrender to King Wilhelm I, who was present there together with Bismarck and Moltke. Exaltation spread amongst the Prussian camp, and Bismarck accepted the surrender in the name of his monarch, appointing Moltke for further negotiations of the French surrender.

A painting depicting Bismarck's (right) stern talk with Napoleon III (left) after the Battle of Sedan. Source: https://commons.wikimedia.org

Having muscled himself as the commander of the Army of Châlons, it was up to Wimpffen to hammer out the capitulation terms with Moltke. The French general pleaded for leniency, asking for an "honorable capitulation." Moltke refused. He wouldn't allow the French troops to march away with their equipment and military honors. It would be ludicrous, as they were sure to fight them again. Bismarck shared his views. To assure Wimpffen's compliance with total capitulation, Moltke showed him a diagram of Prussian battery positions, stating that a force of over 200,000 men and 700 guns would continue their attack tomorrow morning if the French refused. Wimpffen accepted immediately. To protect his reputation, he also forced other French generals to sign a note of compliance to the terms of surrender. Only Napoleon III didn't sign. Instead, he rode to Wilhelm I the next morning, imploring him personally for leniency. Before he was able to present his case, Bismarck gave him a longwinded lesson, leaving the emperor without any words for the king.

In a matter of hours, the capitulation was signed, adding another 83,000 French prisoners, raising the total tally to 104,000. The entire Army of Châlons, 130,000 strong, was removed from the war.

The emperor was captured, and the road to Paris was undefended. France was in a dreadful position overall, as no proper fighting force was available to an already wavering government in Paris. The Prussians' success was paid with only about nine thousand German casualties. Those losses were lessened by the fact that tens of thousands of Chassepot rifles and hundreds of artillery guns were now in German hands.

The captured French conscripts were slowly shipped toward Prussia and were held in rather abysmal conditions. It was only upon seeing those columns that the defenders at Metz realized no relief was coming. Bazaine ordered no more sorties, only small-scale scavenging missions. The Army of Metz slowly withered away as starvation and sickness began taking their toll. Such inactivity was a relief to Moltke, who sent his two armies from Sedan to Paris. They reached the French capital on September 15th. The Army of the Meuse began spreading around the city from the north, while the Third Army wrapped around it from the south. By September 19th, Paris was cut off, surrounded by roughly 240,000 German troops. Regardless, the city wasn't in much danger from a full-blown attack. It bolstered strong defensive forts, which were aided by makeshift barricades and fortifications and covered by more than 1,300 guns. Furthermore, it had a garrison of about 400,000 to 450,000 men; however, only less than 100,000 were trained soldiers. Others were members of the national guard, meaning they lacked discipline or proper training. Even so, together, they proved enough of a deterrent to the Germans but were unable to mount any serious breakthrough.

With the sieges of Paris and Metz, the war entered a military stalemate. The French were unable to mount any kind of counteroffensive; even the forces gathered in the rest of the country were momentarily lacking in training and supplies. On the other hand, the German forces were strung out, unable to storm the formidable forces that tied down almost all of their fighting capacities. Additionally, both sides had troubles with supplies, most notably food. The besieged French forces were in a slightly worse position, yet the Germans weren't faring much better, as the countryside they were encamped on was quickly depleted. The worsening autumn weather only added to the troubles, as illnesses began plaguing both sides. Thus, for a while, the war shifted back to being a political issue more than a military one. Bismarck was back in the spotlight.

Despite the major victories and more than favorable odds, securing peace wouldn't be easy. Bismarck and Moltke believed that Napoleon would slip away from Sedan, allowing them to pursue a quick peace. Instead, he was captured. In a matter of days, the Second French Empire crumbled. On September 4th, when news of Sedan reached the capital, riots erupted almost immediately. The masses wanted to oust the Bonaparte regime. Politicians Léon Gambetta and Jules Favre, backed by General Louis Trochu, proclaimed a provisional government. The so-called Government of National Defense was plagued by numerous political issues. First of all, its leaders weren't properly elected, and almost immediately, it split into two opposing factions. On one side were the moderates, representing the rural population and better-off social classes, who were in favor of gaining peace as quickly as possible. On the other side were the radicals, which mostly contained the poorer urban working classes, who were imbued with nationalism and antimonarchism. They wanted a "maximum war"; in other words, they wanted the Germans to pay in blood.

An 1860s photograph of Favre (top) and Gambetta (bottom). Source: https://commons.wikimedia.org

The provisional government tried to find some middle ground, but that proved difficult. The rural population wanted nothing but peace, while the proletarian movement in Paris began campaigning for *La Commune*. They wanted to establish a new order of shared wealth and property led by local communes. In short, it was the first actual, active seeds of communist ideology in political life. The new government had to suppress such movements, leaving Paris in almost constant chaos of protests and riots. The commotion and the advancing Prussian troops prompted the republican government to split itself. Trochu, its provisional head and commander of the Parisian forces, stayed in the capital with Gambetta, while Favre and a "government delegation" went to Tours on September 13th. There, they would organize the rest of France in the upcoming war effort.

The commotion caused by the fall of the empire caused Bismarck substantial problems. He had hoped to finish the war before the neutral nations stepped in to intervene, but he wasn't going to settle for mere monetary settlement. He demanded Alsace and Lorraine from the provisional government. It was to be a punishment for the war as well as past humiliations that the French had caused the German people. Furthermore, Bismarck's demands were backed up by the Prussians' historical claim on the regions, as they were once part of the Holy Roman Empire. Favre refused such peace offers, claiming that France wouldn't yield an inch of its lands to the Germans. His counteroffer was a large indemnity and part of the French fleet; he was even willing to negotiate about ceding some colonies outside Europe. Bismarck wasn't interested. Thus, the two sides were locked in the talks, neither willing to compromise on their stance.

With both Favre and Bismarck stubbornly set in their ways, they tried to find other political means to achieve them. France sent their ambassadors around Europe and talked with foreign representatives in Paris. They tried to persuade other nations to put pressure on the Germans to accept a less favorable peace treaty. In the cases of

Russia and Italy, the French diplomats tried to tempt them with territorial gains in the Balkans and Rome, respectively. In the cases of Austria and Britain, they dangled the threatened balance of power if Prussia became too powerful. However, they weren't able to make any real allies, apart from vague support from Italy. The French diplomatic position was hardened by the lack of a strong and unified government, leaving many to wonder if the current leaders even had control over the nation. Furthermore, some of the opponents of the provisional government actually traveled around the continent, spreading the "red scare" of impending revolutions, while members of earlier dynasties, like the Bourbons and Orléans, loomed around the border, waiting for their opportunity.

Of course, Bismarck wasn't going to sit around and wait. Prussia also used diplomacy to maintain the neutrality of other European nations. However, his main concern was how to force the French to peace. Being a keen politician, he began plotting on two fronts. On the one hand, he tried negotiating with Bazaine. The marshal was offered liberation from Metz to lead a counter-coup with Prussian support, with the aim of either reestablishing the Bonaparte regime in some kind of capacity or even establishing his own personal dictatorship. These topics were also brought to the empress, who had escaped to Britain in early September, and to Napoleon himself. However, these bore no fruit, as both Bazaine and the Bonapartes wanted too much leeway and separation from the Germans. Nevertheless, Bazaine's willingness to negotiate in such a capacity and his refusal to recognize the new republican government just added to the image of his betrayal of the French people.

Bismarck's other front was trying to negotiate a nationwide election across France, including the return of Alsace and Lorraine, with the Government of National Defense. He hoped that these would provide a more stable and widely accepted government, one that would be able to accept Prussian demands. That offer was rebuffed, as it implied the continued German occupation of France.

Nevertheless, by declining to hold an election, regardless of Prussian participation in holding them, the provisional government's credibility was hurt. To some, it was a sign of yearning to hold power while disregarding the will of the people. As time passed, France was slowly losing its unity. Paris was experiencing increasing revolutionary fervor, which expanded, to some extent, to other major cities. The rural population, usually more monarchical orientated, began feeling too much exhaustion with the burden of war as well as resentment toward the republic. Overall, the government in Tours was losing its grip over France.

Political uncertainty quickly eroded the idea of a diplomatic solution to the war. By early October, it was clear that the war needed a more militaristic resolution. Both sides prepared for renewed combat operations, though the negotiations never fully stopped. Talks would be done with the sound of guns and rifles in the background.

Chapter 7 –The Last Stand: The Road to Peace and the End of the War

As the autumn began to take hold, the hostilities in the French countryside would resume. Taking advantage of the relative lull on the front line, the provisional government managed to gather some troops in the south. In contrast, the relative inactivity of the Parisian defenders allowed Moltke to detach several divisions under the command of Bavarian General Ludwig von der Tann to combat the new threat.

Moltke's military solution to a political stalemate was to actively search and destroy French relief armies, which had the added bonus of safeguarding the ongoing siege of Paris. Tann commanded the Bavarian I Corps and was aided by some Prussian infantry and cavalry divisions. It was a detachment roughly fifty thousand men strong, and it traveled south toward Orléans and the Loire River. Along the way, they met little resistance, mostly some local partisan troops. These kinds of troops plagued the entire German army. However, their actions were more a nuisance than a threat. Even some of the locals refused to help them, fearing Prussian retribution. Regardless of the irregular resistance, for the detached corps, the march southward was initially a welcome rest. Unlike the depleted surroundings of Paris, this region was largely intact, and the men managed to find plentiful supplies.

By October 9th, Tann's troops arrived just north of Orléans, where they were welcomed by a small French force under the command of General Joseph de La Motte-Rouge. Adding to the problems of numbers, most of the French soldiers were part of the national guard, meaning they had little to no training. Only a smaller number of them were properly trained; some had been recalled from their station in Rome, some were part of the French Foreign Legionnaires, and some were the scraps of the regular troops. The mostly untrained and inexperienced French corps was no match to the Germans. In the initial clash, they were quickly routed, while the Germans used their cavalry to flank them. Motte-Rouge tried to position his troops defensively at Orléans, but when they were engaged by the German artillery, they stood no chance. On October 11th, the French corps scrambled. Their losses were incomparable with the Germans, as no less than four thousand trained soldiers were killed or captured—exactly those troops France couldn't afford to lose. In contrast, the Germans lost maybe around nine hundred men.

Once Orléans was captured, Tann was faced with a problem. Pursuing the enemy wasn't an option, as more troops were gathering in much larger numbers farther south. If he ventured too far, he would be too exposed. The detached army already felt exposed, but Moltke rebuffed any ideas of retreat. Thus, the Germans began reinforcing their defenses at Orléans, arming themselves with Chassepots to better their defensive capabilities. They also gathered as much food as they could, plundering the region to prepare for the upcoming winter. These were sometimes masked by terms of "requisition," some vague deals that the French government would later cover with their expenses, or threat of violence. The pressure of war was spreading across France, which only added to the defeatist atmosphere. More and more peasants wanted nothing more than peace.

Moltke ordered Tann, who had been left to guard the forces besieging Paris, to suppress any organized resistance from the south. The Bavarian general complied, and after a few days, he dispatched some of his troops to some of the surrounding towns. Those were conquered relatively easily, as they were inadequately defended. To ensure collaboration, the Germans showed no mercy. They maimed prisoners, shot suspected partisans, and burned villages and towns to the ground. They even took civilians as hostages. After securing the region, Moltke then redirected Tann toward Tours. He was to follow the Loire to the second capital. There, Gambetta, who had managed to sneak out of Paris on a hot air balloon, was taking over control of the French war effort. It seemed Moltke and Bismarck wanted to finish the war before winter truly came and made the lives of their soldiers miserable.

However, the French weren't going to sit idly. General Louis Aurelle de Paladines was given command of Motte-Rouge's XV Corps, which was aided by newly gathered troops. That fighting force now numbered about sixty thousand soldiers, though most of them were still untrained national guardsmen whose discipline was almost nonexistent. Nevertheless, his force, if combined with other troops massing in the south, could possibly rise up to challenge Moltke's siege of Paris. To achieve that, Aurelle needed to take hold of defendable crossroads closer to the capital, where he could be safe while training his conscripts to become proper soldiers. The only real solution was to retake Orléans. Along with other remaining high-ranking officers, plans for that action were made, while Gambetta and his government worked hard to procure any kind of weapons and artillery from Europe and even from the US. Thus, these new French forces were being armed with thousands of Enfield, Remington, and Springfield rifles, as well as the reworked

1822 model muskets. These troops were also armed with repurposed naval guns.

While the new forces in the south of France were preparing to challenge the German forces on the battlefield, Bazaine's Army of Metz was slowly rotting away. His attempts to strike a bargain with Bismarck led nowhere, and even his troops caught wind of the covert communication. His own soldiers were either swept by apathy or anger, feeling personally betrayed. Even worse, many were suffering from starvation and diseases, and their equipment decayed in the bad weather, as most soldiers neglected to maintain them. By mid-October, this formidable fighting force was that only on paper, as in reality, it was unable for any concrete action. The soldiers began sustaining themselves on horse meat, but those supplies quickly ran out. Facing complete starvation and helped by the fact that the Prussians refused to take in more than a handful of deserters per day, Bazaine had no other way out than to surrender.

A picture of Prussian troops occupying one of Metz's forts after the French surrendered. Source: https://commons.wikimedia.org

On October 29th, the Army of Metz capitulated. Prince Friedrich Karl offered Bazaine a surrender with full military honors, allowing the French to exit the fort armed with banners and marching music.

Bazaine refused, ordering his men to simply stack their deteriorated rifles and wait for the Germans to take them away. Furthermore, he willingly gave up all their flags and standards, another controversial act, as most units preferred them destroyed rather than captured by the enemy. Regardless of the shameful conclusion of the siege of Metz, where Bazaine literally ran away from his men, France, in the end, lost another 140,000 men, including thousands of much-needed officers, while also giving up roughly 600 guns and more than 200,000 rifles. The tally of captured French soldiers went up to about 250,000, including 4 marshals, 140 generals, and 10,000 officers. When the news broke, another wave of violent outbursts swept France, especially in the capital. Yet, Parisians also reverted to dark humor, joking that at least Bazaine and MacMahon had finally joined forces. Regardless of the rage and despair shared by the masses, Gambetta and the provisional government in Tours refused to back down. They were determined to continue the struggles with the troops they could muster in the south.

Upon realizing that he was outnumbered, Tann remained at Orléans, perhaps waiting for some reinforcements from Metz. However, the French weren't going to wait, and in early November, they began their march toward him. Their plan was to group all their forces, which would number more than 100,000, and envelop the Germans from the south and the west. Yet, unlike his French counterparts, Tann wasn't going to wait for them to arrive. He decided to gamble, taking twenty thousand of his soldiers and marching to meet Aurelle's corps of sixty thousand. He hoped his better-trained troops would be able to outmaneuver and outperform the unruly French recruits. On November 9th, the two forces collided at Coulmiers, some ten miles (seventeen kilometers) west of Orléans. Tann's initial guess proved right, as, despite their numerical advantage, the French were unable to breach his thin lines. Yet, with so few soldiers, the Germans were pinned down and too weak to attack even though they had the advantage. To make matters worse, they were being rained on by the French artillery, which, though improvised from naval guns, began employing some Prussian tactics. Thus, it became a war of attrition, something Tann wasn't going to win. To prevent a major disaster, he yielded his position by nightfall, though he managed to repulse all French attacks.

A 1911 illustration of the French celebrating their victory at Coulmiers.
Source: https://commons.wikimedia.org

By the next day, Aurelle arrived at Orléans to find that the Germans had retreated completely. Tann withdrew north to Angerville, halfway between his former position and Paris. This angered Moltke, who soon removed him from his commanding post. He gave it to Grand Duke Friedrich of Mecklenburg-Schwerin and reinforced the army with several Prussian corps and divisions from the Second Army. By mid-November, the forces from Metz were redeployed, following vaccinations against smallpox, which had begun to plague the soldiers due to their filthy living conditions. This new defensive German line was spread from Troyes to Chartres, covered by roughly 150,000 soldiers. Their orders were to protect the besiegers of Paris from any French attacks from the southwest. Against them stood a divided French force with an additional three newly formed corps. Combined with irregular militia and partisans, the French Army had swollen up to about 250,000 men, though most of them were still untrained.

However, Aurelle had no intention of massing an offensive. Instead, he entrenched at Orléans, largely ignoring requests for action from Gambetta and his government in Tours. He reasoned that the troops needed to be trained to become a functional army capable of serious combat. The cold winter weather and snow also helped in his resolve to stay in the warmth of a city. Despite the promises of freeing Paris, which had been made by the provisional government, this action was sensible. After the losses of almost all of the regular army, the French forces could survive only by being defensive. On the other hand, Grand Duke Friedrich was largely unaware of how bad the shape of the French Army was. Thus, he split his forces into several defensive positions while marching toward the French XXI Corps stationed at Le Mans. It was a preemptive strike at a force of only thirty-five thousand men that could, at some point, possibly threaten the besiegers of Paris from the west. However, the commander of the French corps retreated without giving battle. By then, the French had finally managed to bypass the lack of intelligence-gathering missions of their cavalry, which had plagued them in the early stages of the war. Now, they were relying on partisans and locals to gather information on Prussian movements and positions.

Through that intelligence network, the leaders of the provisional government learned that yet another batch of Prussian reinforcements, under Prince Friedrich Karl, was arriving from Metz. Gambetta and his republican high command felt that an early strike was the only solution, as they still had some numerical superiority against the southern German armies. Their main fear was that it was only a matter of time before these German troops grouped and advanced to Tours. Thus, they forced Aurelle to act, despite his hesitations. He gathered his troops and pushed to Beaune-la-Rolande. It was just twenty-five miles (forty kilometers) northeast of Orléans and guarded by three Prussian brigades. They were only meant to be an early warning for an attack, not a real line of German defense. So, Aurelle felt his rowdy army of 60,000 men and 140 guns could take on 9,000 Prussians with half as much artillery.

The two sides clashed on November 28th, but the French failed to exploit their superiority in numbers. Their attacks were repulsed by a remarkably disciplined and stubborn Prussian defense. Realizing they had no reserves or much supplies, they waited for each French advance to get to less than two hundred yards away before opening precise fire. All the while, they endured heavy artillery bombardments and mitrailleuse fire. The untrained French recruits were no match to the well-trained battle-hardened Prussians, who broke off the French offensive by the end of the day. The disparity in the quality of troops is exemplified through the casualties at Beaune-la-Rolande. The Germans had only 850, while the French lost roughly 8,000 men in a battle where they outnumbered the enemies more than six to one.

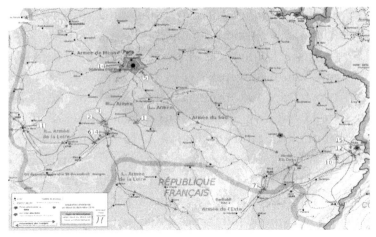

A map depicting rough army movements, positions, and the front lines from December 1870 to January 1871 (note – the French eastern border depicts Alsace and Lorraine as already part of Germany). Source: https://commons.wikimedia.org

As if that loss wasn't enough for Aurelle and Gambetta, they proceeded with yet another attack. They sent another fresh corps at the German positions in Loigny, just north of Orléans, on December 2nd. This battle was between armies of equal size, roughly thirty-five thousand each, with both sides deployed in long skirmish lines on an open field that offered little protection against enemy fire or artillery shrapnel. A rather primitive shootout lasted the entire day, ending in a Prussian victory. The French lost seven thousand men, including captured, while the Germans suffered roughly four thousand casualties. It was a much closer call for the Germans simply because the open field suited the French longer-ranged rifles much better, yet they weren't able to exploit that. Furthermore, the harshness of winter caused troubles on both sides. However, the loss at Loigny proved to be the final straw for the greenhorns in the French Army.

Losing their morale and troubled by cold and hunger, the French were losing their willingness to oppose the Germans. Realizing that, Moltke ordered that that Orléans needed to be retaken. Prince Friedrich Karl amassed his troops and marched to it on December

3rd. The remaining French forces put up some resistance, yet they slowly yielded their positions under heavy artillery fire. The fight lasted for two days, but in the end, there wasn't much fight left in the French Army, and it descended into a chaotic rout. Aurelle's army split into two halves, one north and one south of the Loire. The French general ordered his troops to retreat farther south, leaving the ones north of the river on their own. In the end, Friedrich Karl recaptured Orléans, losing only about 1700 of his men in the process, while the French lost around 20,000, with 18,000 being prisoners. With that, any hope of relieving Paris was gone, and the provisional government retreated farther south, making Bordeaux its new informal capital.

Aurelle was relieved of duty, but the army remained split in two. The southern half was placed under the command of General Charles Bourbaki, who managed to slip away from Metz during the siege. His troops retreated toward Brogues. The northern part of the army was given to General Antoine Chanzy, who retreated toward Tours. At Beaugency, he tried to regroup his panicked soldiers. He gathered a disorganized army of about 100,000 men, with the bad weather only further hampering his efforts. These two factors made his army rather immobile, preventing him from moving his men to the left bank of the Loire and head over to reunite with Bourbaki. This allowed for a much smaller German force, with less than thirty thousand soldiers, to engage him in combat, which lasted for several days. Chanzy hoped that he could budge the Prussians by attacking them while waiting for some help from Bourbaki. By around December 10th, Moltke ordered Friedrich Karl to reinforce the advance on Beaugency. Realizing no help was coming, this left Chanzy with only the possibility of retreat. He headed west to Le Mans. The French managed to slip away mostly because the Germans weren't too keen on pursuing them, as cold weather and fatigue caught up with them. Similar conditions, aided with the demoralization from defeat, also bogged down

Bourbaki's army. His soldiers simply refused to comply with the orders to move out. For a while, the southern front went quiet.

While the two sides clashed on the banks of the Loire, the Parisian front also lit up. Morale sank after the surrender of Metz, while the lack of supplies put added pressure on the Parisians. This prompted Trochu to act. After being informed of Aurelle's movements in late November, he and his generals planned a sortie on November 28th. It was supposed to strike southwest of Paris, simultaneously cutting off communications from Prussian headquarters in Versailles with the troops in the east of the city, while forming a bridge toward the troops advancing from the Loire and gathering supplies from the German besiegers. However, the engineers failed to mount pontoon bridges in time, derailing the attack and pushing it back to the 30th, giving time for the besiegers to prepare. The French tried to mask the main line of the sortie with a diversion, but the Prussians weren't fooled. They greeted their main attack at Villiers and Champigny, the southeastern outskirts of Paris, just south of the Marne. The battle lasted until December 4th, with the French clinging for longer than reasonable on Gambetta's vague promises of relief from the Loire.

The failed breakthrough cost the Parisians twelve thousand men, most of whom were the trained soldiers spearheading the assault; the number of trained men was already lacking among the defenders of Paris, which made this blow even harder to suffer. Regardless of the loss and creeping hunger, Paris refused to surrender. The provisional government refused as well, as Gambetta was resolute on continuing the fight, even after the Loire army was functionally knocked out of the war. This posed a new problem for the German occupiers, who had hoped these victories would finally force France into submission. On the one hand, Bismarck continuously worried about the neutral powers stepping in to rein in Prussia. On the other, prolonged war and the harsh winter continued to wear down Moltke's troops and supplies. The two of them argued and disagreed on what would be the proper solution for this French stubbornness.

Unusually, the politician argued for a more violent plan. Bismarck argued all they had to do was exert unbearable pressure on the civilians, forcing the provisional government to settle for his terms. Thus, he advocated relocating heavy guns and mortars to bombard Paris, regardless of the civilian population. His willingness to harm the French nation as a whole only increased due to the actions of French partisans and irregulars. Those forces, numbering maybe thirty thousand to forty thousand in total, weren't a match to the Prussian soldiers, but they constantly harassed the Prussians while they were on the move, disrupting supply lines by demolishing railways and bridges. This nuisance forced Moltke to separate about 100,000 men to guard shipments headed to the front lines. As soldiers had a hard time dealing with the elusive partisans, who were without uniforms, some simply began shooting at anyone even vaguely suspected of insurgent activities. It was a gruesome reprisal supported by Bismarck as another way of pressuring the French. Furthermore, he used reports of the partisans killing and torturing Prussian prisoners as more proof that they shouldn't show mercy to the civilians.

In contrast, Moltke was far less bloodthirsty. He wanted to starve out the French as they had done at Metz. He argued that transporting mortars and heavy guns, as well as their ammunition, would only add to the stress of resupplying the Prussian forces. Furthermore, he suggested that harming civilians en masse would only infuriate other countries, turning them firmly against Prussia. Not least, Moltke felt this kind of action wasn't very civilized or in the proper military and German spirit. Bismarck had no morality issues like those. He thought that brutality was justified to end the war before some unforeseen event, be it foreign intervention or reversal of battle fortunes, weakened Prussia's negotiating position. Bismarck dubbed this the "wartime political effort" (*Politik im*

Krieg), where the military was working toward a political goal. This debate between the chancellor and field marshal was settled by the minister of war. Roon sided with Bismarck, swaying the king at the same time. The Prussians were to bombard Paris.

While the heavy guns were still being deployed, the Parisians attempted another breakthrough on December 21ˢᵗ. It was a sign of desperation, as it was now aimed toward the north, hoping to connect with the so-called Army of the North that was stationed in Lille. However, these thirty-five thousand men were soldiers only on paper, even according to their commanding officer, who characterized them as an unarmed and untrained group lacking proper officers. Their futility is further corroborated by the fact that the Prussians almost ignored their existence, satisfied with isolating them from the rest of France. Regardless, this sortie was rebuffed by the Germans with ease, while the Parisian defenders were starting to run low on sufficiently trained troops to send on such missions. Their low morale was soon to get even worse, for, by the last days of 1870, the Prussians finally deployed over seventy heavy guns and began their bombardment. Their primary targets were forts on the outskirts of Paris, which protected the city from invaders, but some shells managed to hit civilian targets, including hospitals, churches, schools, and private homes. Reports of noncombatant casualties began to seep in. However, German shells weren't a primary cause of civilian deaths. By January, up to four thousand citizens were dying weekly from starvation and cold.

Civilian parts of Paris that were damaged by Prussian artillery. Source: https://commons.wikimedia.org

While the Parisians suffered, Chanzy was entrenched at Le Mans with his army of about 100,000. He sent smaller regiments to harass the Second Army while the rest worked on fortifications. Along the way, the provisional government worked on reorganizing and resupplying its army, trying to increase its combat effectiveness. Moltke noticed that, and on New Year's Day, he ordered Prince Friedrich Karl to mobilize his army westward and deal a final strike to the Army of the Loire. The prince complied, gathering about seventy-three thousand of his men, and slowly advanced toward Le Mans, reaching it on January 10th. The men showed signs of fatigue over the long campaign and cold weather, so the initial German attack was rather uncoordinated and slow, allowing Chanzy's defenses to stave off the attackers for a day. Yet, the very next day, a bold advance surprised the inexperienced national guard regiments, causing panic and routing them. Once it began, Chanzy couldn't stop it. His soldiers were cold, wet, hungry, and sleepless, lacking any will to fight. The army virtually disintegrated, and the fighting broke off on January 12th. Chanzy and a small part of his troops managed to slip away. According to some estimations, he lost about twenty-five thousand men, both in casualties and prisoners, but up to twice as many deserted during the retreat. Regardless of how many men he retained under his command, that group ceased to be an effective fighting force. Soldiers abandoned much of their arms and ammunition, and morale was at an all-time low.

With Chanzy's demise and all Parisian breakout attempts failing, Gambetta turned his attention to the eastern theater of the war. By late December, he ordered Bourbaki's army to march toward Dijon, where a single Baden Corps was holding the city. Gambetta's idea was to strike the Prussian flank from the southeast, in the region between Dijon and Belfort, and hit the German supply lines. It was a reasonable last attempt at doing anything, especially since the small Army of the Vosges operated in the region. It was led by the famous Giuseppe Garibaldi, an old Italian revolutionary general, and consisted mostly of foreign volunteers, for example, Poles, Irish, Spanish, Americans, and, of course, Italians. These were usually somewhat experienced and trained men, but the unit lacked overall cohesion and discipline, with too many internal squabbles and debates. The volunteer army was operational since early November, with no more than twenty thousand men, but it made little impression on the course of the war. Yet, if that force was to unite and cooperate with Bourbaki's 110,000 men, together, they could seriously threaten the German rear.

Of course, Moltke was aware of that; thus, he formed a new German "Army of the South" from three Prussian corps and sent them in pursuit. The goal was to destroy France's last remnants of a field army. However, Bourbaki proved to be less of a threat than originally expected. His army advanced quite slowly, encumbered with supply issues, demoralization, and the cold. Regardless, the German corps holding the city withdrew without a fight in late December and began its retreat eastward. This was done because the primary task of the Badenese was to safeguard the siege of Belfort, a fortified town on the southern edges of the Vosges. Holding ground against a numerically superior enemy at Dijon, which was more than 80 miles (128 kilometers) west of Belfort, seemed unwise, as the men were far from any possible reinforcements and were vulnerable to encirclement. Thus, the Germans rolled all the way back to the Lisaine River and the fortified town of Héricourt, with the French slowly trailing behind them. The hesitation to engage the Baden Corps infuriated Bourbaki's superiors, and it made the Germans question if he was even going to relieve the siege of Belfort at all.

Regardless, the two sides finally clashed when the French attacked on January 15th. By then, Héricourt was fortified by the Badenese. The attackers crossed the frozen river that separated the two sides, and a three-day battle ensued, filled with heavy fighting, artillery exchanges, and harsh weather. The French had some limited success at certain points, taking parts of the German outer posts, but the defenders gave stiff resistance to their advances. By the end of the 17th, Bourbaki disengaged, losing about 8,000 men, while the Baden Corps suffered about 1,600 casualties. The French "eastern army" remained functional, yet with the German Army of the South approaching, it wasn't going to pose much of a threat anymore.

It was becoming obvious even to the fiercest French proponents of a defiant resistance that the war was lost. Trochu, who corresponded with Moltke about surrendering in early January, agreed upon a last desperate sortie on January 19th, but that attempt failed like the others, just adding to French casualty numbers. The very next day, Paris descended into riots, with the workers gathering on the streets, demanding the formation of communes and the removal of Trochu. They even began showing signs of distrust toward the republic. Such developments finally pushed Favre to travel to Versailles on January 23rd to begin negotiations with

Bismarck. On January 26th, they signed an armistice, officially ending the hostilities on January 28th. The treaty stipulated that Paris had to surrender, giving up both its armaments and fortifications; in return, the Germans would immediately send in rations. Afterward, France had until February 19th to elect a national assembly, which would then ratify peace on German terms. If the assembly refused, the Prussians would descend upon the disarmed and exposed French nation.

The last remnants of the French Army surrendering their arms at the Swiss border. Source: https://commons.wikimedia.org

Thus, for most of the French, the war ended on January 28th, 1871, yet Favre and Gambetta still had illusions about Bourbaki's army. Thus, Favre excluded the region where he was held up, near the Swiss border, from the armistice. The Government of National Defense still hoped that a miraculous victory by those forces could better their negotiating position. Instead, Bourbaki tried and failed to take his own life after facing numerous accusations over his leadership, and the army fell into disarray. Men were cold, hungry, and without equipment. Instead of fighting, they withdrew beyond the Swiss border on February 1st, factually ending the last flicker of the Franco-Prussian War.

Chapter 8 – Life Goes On: The Aftermath of the Franco-Prussian War

Though the armistice ended the fighting, factually finishing the war, it still had to legally be concluded through a peace treaty. That meant weeks of negotiations, with the French trying to stave off German thirst for vengeance.

The peace talks began in a much different balance of power than anyone in Europe had expected, including Bismarck and Moltke. France was at a low point that it hadn't seen for centuries, shamed by a disgraceful military defeat, a poor economy, and their land in ruins, not to mention the chaotic political scene. As agreed in the armistice, a nationwide election was held with the help of the Germans on February 8th. Unsurprisingly, the most successful were the candidates who promoted peace and liberty, so a majority of the seats in the National Assembly went to rural monarchists and conservatives, while the moderate republicans held less than 30 percent. Radical republicans even got votes, and surprisingly, there was also a handful of Bonapartists who gained seats. The new leader of what was now the French Third Republic was Adolphe Thiers, an old republican who helped to create the Second Republic in 1848. Thiers retained most of the ministers from the provisional government, including Favre. Gambetta, a continued proponent of the war, remained outside of it.

A legally constituted government gave Thiers legitimacy to negotiate with Bismarck, but the elections were far from being a soothing factor as some hoped. France remained deeply divided, with brewing discontent across all major cities. Like always, that feeling was strongest in Paris, where the working classes remained radical and prone to outbursts and riots. At the time, Bordeaux remained as the government headquarters, but Thiers wanted to regain control over the capital, which held to its anti-governmental sentiments. This led to a confrontation, sparked by the regular army trying to take a handful of obsolete guns left by the Prussians at the Parisian forts. On March 18th, the Paris Commune was established when the revolutionary Communards, as they called themselves, took control of the city once the army withdrew. This sparked similar but much less successful attempts to establish communes in other major cities, such as Lyon or Marseille. Regardless, the nation was entrenched in what can be characterized as a civil war. Such instability only worsened Thiers's negotiation position. It reduced his internal political strength as well as diplomatic reach, as it made most of the European monarchies quite wary of the Parisian radicals.

A barricade of the Paris Commune, preparing to defend their rebellion.
Source: https://commons.wikimedia.org

Opposed to them stood the victorious and, more importantly, united Germany, just as Bismarck had planned. As he had expected and predicted, a defensive war against the French aroused nationalist feelings among the Germanic people. Nevertheless, Bismarck knew that he needed more than just public support, which, of course, wasn't spread equally among the independent Germanic states. On the one hand, Bavaria was the most opposed to the idea of unification, with such sentiments coming from a wider public as well as its ruler, King Ludwig II. On the other side of the spectrum, the Grand Duchy of Baden was wholly behind the idea, and it even petitioned to be admitted to the North German Confederation after 1866. Thus, as far back as September 1870, Bismarck had begun a series of talks and conferences with representatives from Bavaria, Baden, Hessen, and Württemberg. Through these, they agreed upon details of how these states would be incorporated into the newly formed German Confederation in November, creating the first step toward formal unification. These agreements were framed as more of federal agreements, with four independent Germanic countries retaining some sovereignty, for example, an independent post, railway, and army. Furthermore, it was an agreement between the North German Confederation and those states; thus, it didn't change the already existing relations between Prussia and the other already assimilated countries.

The next step was taken in the federal assembly, where in early December, a motion was proposed for reinstituting the German Empire and offering the imperial title to Prussian King Wilhelm I. To give this motion more strength, Bismarck arranged that it would be proposed by none other than Ludwig II. In fact, to secure his support, the chancellor arranged that the Bavarian king would be paid 300,000 marks annually from the so-called "Guelph Fund," a secretly seized Hanoverian state treasury that came into Prussian hands in 1866. It was nothing less than a bribe, and it remained a secret for a long time. Regardless, Bismarck continued his political machinations, and by January 1871, the proposed unification was put to the vote in the parliaments of the south Germanic states. As expected, the Bavarians were the most opposed, yet the decree was passed on January 21ˢᵗ, with a margin of only two votes.

A later rendition of the proclamation of the German Empire in the Hall of Mirrors at Versailles. Source: https://commons.wikimedia.org

However, Bismarck was sure the unification would be accepted; thus, on January 18th, he organized the official proclamation of the German Empire, or *Deutsches Kaiserreich*, sometimes also erroneously named the Second Reich. It was held in the Hall of Mirrors in Versailles, giving the event a double meaning. The date was the anniversary of when the Kingdom of Prussia was officially formed in 1701, and holding the entire ceremony in the most famous French palace was, of course, an exhibition of domination over their defeated enemies. It wasn't a grand ceremony, as most generals and officers showed up in their combat uniforms, and it was also riddled with problems for Bismarck. For example, Wilhelm wanted the title of Emperor of Germany, but his chancellor secured him the title of German Emperor, a title that Wilhelm thought had less grandeur and tradition. Regardless, the ceremony proceeded with everyone referring to him as simply Emperor or Kaiser Wilhelm. Bismarck saw this moment as his own crowning achievement, but accounts state that the overall atmosphere was cold and rather rigid, without a proper celebratory feel to it.

Despite the fact that most of the other European powers weren't too keen on the creation of a new empire in the heart of the continent, they did nothing to stop it. Shocked or impressed with the German victories over France, they deemed it unwise to interfere. With their internal and external positions so different, the French and the Germans began negotiating for peace on February 21st. The new empire was represented by Bismarck, while Thiers and Favre negotiated in the name of the French. The talks, held in Versailles, were tough and exhausting, especially for the Frenchmen. Bismarck demanded harsh terms, most notably the annexation of Alsace and Lorraine, but also an indemnity of six billion francs in gold. Those terms wouldn't just humiliate France; it would cripple the country. The reparations would be hard to pay on its own, but the two provinces the Germans demanded were also the industrial and economic heart of France, holding 20 percent of its mining and steel production potential.

Of course, Thiers tried to work around these issues, but Bismarck wouldn't budge much. This was partially caused by his own feelings toward the French. Furthermore, he believed that, unlike Austria, France would never forgive the Prussians for the victory, no matter how generous the peace terms were. Additionally, he had to account for political pressure. The masses in Germany more or less expected and demanded the annexation of these lands, while even Moltke, Roon, and even Wilhelm were also pressuring him to take as much as possible from the French. To them, it was punishment for all the spilled German blood, although Moltke was also thinking about the defensive needs in future wars. Thus, whenever Thiers tried to negotiate against the demands, Bismarck simply threatened him and France with the continuation of the war. On the other side, Favre and Thiers were aware that the French people would be unsatisfied with anything they could achieve in these talks, which were slowly turning into a dictation of terms. Ultimately, they could do little to sway Bismarck.

When it came to the matter of ceding territories, from the German point of view, the question wasn't "if" but "how much." During the negotiations, there were several contested issues. Roon advocated for annexation all the way to Nancy, yet Bismarck didn't press that far. However, when he considered giving up on Metz, Moltke and other officers were outraged. Initially, Bismarck didn't consider Metz as incredibly valuable, arguing that he would rather take more money and build a new fort a few miles away from it. Yet, the German military personnel were adamant, so he was forced to pressure the French for it. Then they focused on Belfort, which was too much for Thiers. After further arguments, the chancellor said he would consult Wilhelm and Moltke. In the end, it all came down to Moltke's decision, and the field marshal was prepared to back down from Belfort if Thiers would give up four less important villages in Lorraine, which had ten thousand buried Prussians. He also demanded a military entrance and victory parade in Paris. Thiers accepted, as long as the French could retain an important fort, in exchange for this humiliation in the capital.

A photograph of the German victory parade in Paris. Source:
https://commons.wikimedia.org

There were also a lot of negotiations around the indemnity. Thiers initially offered 1.5 billion francs, but Bismarck refused. He wanted more, not only to embarrass the French and get back at them for humiliations in the previous century or so but also to impede their ability to seek retribution. In the end, Bismarck agreed to lower the indemnity to no less than five billion francs to be paid off by 1875. To put it in some perspective, this amounted to about 23 percent of the French annual GDP at the time or around two and a half times the annual government budget. Thiers had no more room for haggling and had to accept. Many foreign observers were shocked and appalled by these reparations, as they went beyond covering the expenses of the war. Some claimed that this could be a dangerous precedent, as it could mean wars might be fought for pure monetary gain. Furthermore, France had to bear a lighter form of German occupation until the indemnity was paid off in full.

Finally, France had to recognize the German unification, the proclamation of the empire, and Wilhelm I as the emperor. This proved to be of little concern to the French when compared to other issues. Apart from that, the two sides agreed upon some technical matters, like the framework of withdrawing from certain regions or forms of payments. Since Bismarck was in a hurry to finish the whole ordeal to focus on building a newly unified nation, he pressured Thiers to accept the peace treaty immediately. Thus, on February 26th, a preliminary peace was signed, but it still had to be ratified by two governments. On March 1st, thirty thousand German troops entered the city, parading for their emperor to the disgust of the Parisians. However, the French government in Bordeaux signed the peace treaty the same day, preventing any further parades. This came as a surprise to the Germans, who expected them to have a lengthy debate in the National Assembly. Thus, by March 3rd, the German troops had evacuated from Paris, though sizable armies remained in the vicinity as part of the occupation force. In Berlin, the newly formed Reichstag, the German assembly, accepted the treaty on March 21st. The formal signing of the agreement was held in Frankfurt on May 10th, formally ending the war between France and Germany.

By then, Thiers was already more concerned with the Paris Commune, which took over control of the capital. Luckily for the French government, the Germans were as hostile to the Communards as they were. Bismarck may have reveled in the glorious mess that France had become, but he saw radical republicanism and emerging communism as a threat to everyone. Thus, he actually went on to provide undirect assistance to France. First, he agreed to allow the French to send eighty thousand troops north of the Loire, which wasn't allowed by the peace treaty. Then, he expedited the release of prisoners, seeking to build up the strength of the French Army to allow it to retake its own capital. Apart from that, they refrained from interfering, as it was a rather delicate issue. Nonetheless, they served as a blockade to the

Communards, as their lines near Paris were closed to any movements from or to the city. Thanks to this, the French Army, with more than 100,000 men, led by the recently released MacMahon, entered the capital on May 21st. Fighting ensued, but some thirty thousand armed revolutionaries were defeated by May 28th, ending the first communist experiment in history to the relief of many, including Bismarck.

With that, peace was finally restored in Europe, at least for a while. On the German side, there were about twenty-eight thousand killed in action and some ninety thousand wounded. Additionally, diseases reportedly took some 12,000 more lives from the German ranks, totaling some 130,000 casualties overall. The French paid for their struggle much more steeply. They had roughly 140,000 dead, with about 45,000 succumbing to various diseases. Furthermore, they had about the same number of wounded, raising their total to roughly 280,000 casualties. On top of that, they had more than 380,000 men imprisoned in Germany, with an additional 95,000 in Switzerland and Belgium; these men had crossed the border to escape the war. These men were, of course, released in the weeks and months after the treaty was signed. On top of that, French civilian casualties should be added; however, there are no clear numbers for them. There are estimates of about twenty thousand civilians losing their lives during the Paris Commune, but the exact number of people during the clash with the Germans is unclear. The initial French reports of civilian casualties put the number at around two thousand or slightly more. However, these seem to be victims of direct military actions, for example, the bombardment of Paris, and excludes people dying from starvation and similar byproducts of war. In reality, French civilian casualties may go up to anywhere between 80,000 to 100,000.

A map of Europe in 1871 with the nations' new borders. The shaded part of France was under temporary German occupation. Source: https://commons.wikimedia.org

Regardless of the losses, both nations had pressing issues to deal with as the dust of the war settled. France was politically fractured, economically devastated, and also suffered from the partial German occupation. To finally liberate itself from the last lingering pressures of the defeat, France strained its finances and paid off the indemnity by September 1873, two years before its due date, ending German military presence on its soil. Despite that, the loss of Alsace and Lorraine remained an issue for many in France. The French economy was slow to recover, as it lost its most vital industrial zones to the Germans, but it managed to get back on its feet in the upcoming years and decades, not without the help of France's vast colonial empire. However, French politics remained somewhat unstable for a long time, as there were many parties, including several monarchists. The Third Republic, as it was called, remained in provisional form until 1875, when a series of laws allowed for the formation of a constitution. With these laws, the government was divided into a two-house legislative system, with both a premier and a president of the republic. Despite that, French politics remained turbulent.

Despite the victory, the newly formed German Empire also had a lot of issues to deal with, especially from Bismarck's perspective. Despite the unification, the new nation was built on a rather unstable federal organization, something that Bismarck worked hard to rectify. Although this never actually changed from a constitutional perspective, the chancellor began equating the laws through several legislative codices. He simultaneously worked on national unity through forced Germanization. This added another bonding factor among the German people in the empire, but it proved to be more than damaging to minorities, like the French in the west, the Danes in the north, and the Poles in the east. On the political scene, Germany proved somewhat stable for a while, with Wilhelm and Bismarck at its helm, but there were plenty of struggles between the various parties. Religious issues were part of these political turbulences, as the Catholic south struggled with the Protestant north. In terms of the economy, Germany flourished due to its rapid industrialization and expanding railways, helped both by the indemnity and acquisition of Alsace and Lorraine. In the years after the war, the German Empire became second only to Great Britain in regards to the greatest economy in Europe, and it was in competition with the United States for the title of world's second-best economy.

As for the leading people of the Franco-Prussian War, they had varying fates. The Bonapartes remained in Great Britain. Napoleon III died a broken man in exile in 1873. His son, Napoleon IV, tried to prove his mettle in war and built up his political credibility. Yet, he lost his life in 1879 in the Zulu War. Thiers remained in office until 1873, but he remained politically present until his death in 1877. He was succeeded by none other than MacMahon, who acted as the French president until 1879. Afterward, he quietly retired from politics. Bazaine was put on trial for treason and convicted to life in prison in 1873, but he escaped to Spain, where he spent his last days. Favre's political career was finished as far back as 1871 when a series of scandals regarding his children from illicit affairs brought him down. Finally, Gambetta continued to play an active political role, serving as the minister of the interior and a premier before he died in an accident in 1882.

On the German side, Emperor Wilhelm I remained on the throne until his death in 1888. Despite vast constitutional power, he remained largely in Bismarck's shadow. Bismarck remained the chancellor of the empire while also serving as a foreign minister and a prime minister of Prussia until 1890, controlling most of German politics until then. He resigned only after clashing with the new emperor, Wilhelm's grandson of the same name, Wilhelm II. Moltke remained the chief of the General Staff until he resigned in 1888, and he then served as a member of the Reichstag until his death in 1891. Roon played several political and military roles immediately after the war, but due to his poor health, he retired quickly afterward, dying in 1879. All three of them were awarded titles after their victory over the French. Moltke and Roon were named counts (*Graf*), while Bismarck was given a princely title (*Fürst*).

A caricature depicting Bismarck choosing suits for many of his roles in German politics. Source: https://commons.wikimedia.org

Thus, by the end of the century, most of the major actors of the war were gone. However, the legacy of the conflict outlasted them, proving to be one of the major events in modern history. Its consequences would certainly be felt by future generations.

Epilogue

The Franco-Prussian War and the peace treaty that ended it proved to be rather controversial, both to their contemporaries and for future politicians and historians. For those observing it, it was a shocking event. It marked a fall of a major power and the birth of another. Furthermore, the peace treaty was seen as one of the harshest in recent history, both in terms of indemnity and territorial losses. On the French side, it birthed revanchism, as the people felt the need to resettle the score with the Germans. On the other side, the Germans began feeling superior, demanding recognition and a place among the world superpowers. Contemporaries also judged that the Franco-Prussian conflict caused a major rebalancing of power in Europe and the world.

The tensions between Germany and France prevailed for decades, and a number of alliances formed around this animosity. Initially, the German Empire, under Bismarck's guidance, proved more adept at this diplomatic game. He organized a pact with two other European empires—Russia and Austria—to prevent the two from joining forces with France to curb the rising power of Germany. He also sought to avoid irritating Britain, which cared little who was dominating the continent as long as it didn't jeopardize the British colonial empire. With France isolated, Europe remained somewhat peaceful.

However, things began to change in the 1880s, as Germany's economic advance began to worry others. Furthermore, the youngest European empire also wanted a place among the colonial powers, joining the infamous Scramble for Africa. Britain took notice of this. Things only took a turn for the worse when Bismarck and Wilhelm I exited the political stage in Germany. The new generation of politicians, led by Emperor Wilhelm II, became increasingly aggressive in their stance. France took this opportunity to ally itself with Britain and Russia, which had changed sides after its pact with Germany expired. On the other side stood Austria, Italy, and the German Empire. All three nations sought to expand their positions on the world stage. The platform was set for the Great War, which would explode in 1914.

This causational link between 1870 and 1914 led many historians and politicians to speculate that one of the major causes for World War I was the harsh treaty imposed on the French, most notably the loss of Alsace and Lorraine. Though there are some truths to this sentiment, as many in France were itching to regain the lost lands, it would be too simplistic a view of the whole situation. It loses track of the longstanding animosity between the two nations while ignoring the fact that the most impactful result of the Franco-Prussian War was the European power system being thrown out of balance.

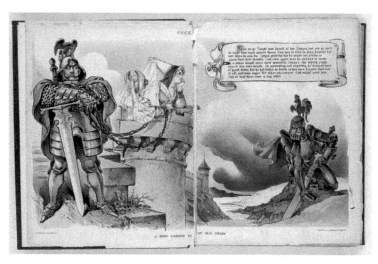

A caricature depicting the French yearning to liberate Alsace and Lorraine.
Source: https://commons.wikimedia.org

Nevertheless, all these consequences of the war are circumstantial, as other factors contributed to it as well. The only legacy solely linked to it was the reform of how the militaries functioned. The entire world was fascinated with Germany's success and decided to copy it to some degree. While some tried to reproduce it to the tiniest tactical detail, like, for example, Russia against the Ottoman Empire in 1878, most were more focused on the grand scale. By 1914, the entire world, from Washington to Tokyo, adopted Moltke's standing General Staff, widespread conscription, rapid and organized mobilization, the use of railways for supply and deployment, a focus on artillery, and the division of the army into smaller, more mobile and interchangeable units. All of these were to become hallmarks of the Great War, at least partially.

However, the imitators and even German successors failed to realize that Moltke's military genius wasn't an independent entity. Most of them neglected the brilliance of Bismarck's politics, and they were unable to recognize that the great German success of 1870 was achieved through a rather turbulent but fruitful partnership between two remarkable persons, who led a motivated and bustling nation in conditions that were perfect for them. Such shortsightedness of later generations led to no less than two major world wars, which, in a simplified view, were essentially an attempt to replicate the Franco-Prussian War on a grander scale. Other nations fared similarly when trying to replicate German success in their confrontations with France.

Conclusion

A short war, like the one fought by the French and the Prussians in 1870, is rarely so impactful in history. Yet the Franco-Prussian War proved to be a turning point in European and world history. It led to a rise of an empire, new military technologies and strategies, and the birth of the "total war" mentality of conflicts. It created more tensions than it solved, such as the first steps toward later major wars. As such, the Franco-Prussian conflict deserves to be studied, as it holds important lessons in military, diplomatic, and political action and thought.

However, instead of trying to learn how to wage war, like many before us did, it is vital to look at this war as a warning. It showcases what happens when nationalism and personal political ambitions leads us forward, as it brings unnecessary conflicts, destruction, and death. The war between France and Prussia was ultimately avoidable, as it was caused by politicians and rulers who didn't see the battlefield, leaving the fighting and dying to the people they were supposedly representing and leading. Worst of all, it only led to the continued circle of vicious violence. That circle was only broken when French and German leaders after World War II decided there was too much death and destruction, not to mention the shame they felt in participating in such events. Thus, it would be much better if we would be able to sense that shame before straying into ultimately futile conflicts.

Lessons of peace are some of the most important that can be taught by history, and hopefully, this guide managed to convey similar sentiments. Yet, reading this shouldn't be an end but rather just a beginning of your curious exploration of the human past, both of this particular topic but also in other areas of history. Let us all learn from the mistakes of the people who came before us, lest we repeat them again.

Here's another book by Captivating History that you might like

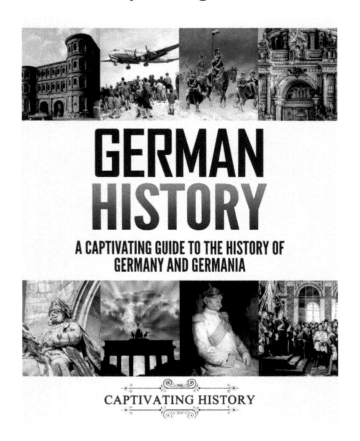

Free Bonus from Captivating History
(Available for a Limited time)

Hi History Lovers!

Now you have a chance to join our exclusive history list so you can get your first history ebook for free as well as discounts and a potential to get more history books for free! Simply visit the link below to join.

Captivatinghistory.com/ebook

Also, make sure to follow us on Facebook, Twitter and Youtube by searching for Captivating History.

Bibliography

Geoffrey Wawro, *The Franco-Prussian War: The German Conquest of France in 1870–1871*, Cambridge University Press, 2003.

Quintin Barry, *The Franco-Prussian War 1870-71 - Volumes 1 & 2*, Helion & Company, 2007.

Stephen Badsey, *The Franco-Prussian War 1870-1871*, 2003.

Michael Howard, *The Franco-Prussian War: The German Invasion of France 1870–1871*, Routledge, 2001.

Jason Philip Coy, *A Brief History of Germany*, Facts on File, 2011.

A, Farmer and A. Stiles, *The Unification of Germany 1815–1919*, Hodder Education, 2007.

Jonathan Steinberg, *Bismarck: A Life*, Oxford University Press, 2011.

Malcolm Crook, *Revolutionary France 1788–1880*, Oxford University Press, 2002.

Melville D. Landon, *The Franco-Prussian War in a Nutshell - A Daily Diary of Diplomacy, Battles, and War Literature*, G. W. Cakleton & Co., 1871.

Michael A. Palmer, *The German War: A Concise History 1859-1945*, Zenith Press, 2010.

H. Hearder, *Europe in the Nineteenth Century 1830-1880*, Longman, 1966.

Robert Gerwarth, *The Bismarck Myth - Weimar Germany and the Legacy of the Iron Chancellor*, Oxford University Press, 2005.

James Retallack, *Imperial Germany 1871–1918*, Oxford University Press, 2008.

Stefan Berger, *A Companion to Nineteenth-Century Europe 1789–1914*, Blackwell Publishing, 2006.

Dennis Showalter, *The wars of German unification*, Bloomsbury academic, 2015.

Otto Pflanze, *Bismarck and the Development of Germany – The Period of Unification 1815-1871*, Princeton University Press, 1963.

A. J. P. Taylor, *Bismarck: The Man and the Statesman*, Vintage Books, 1967.

Count Helmuth Von Moltke, *The Franco-German War of 1870-71*, The Project Gutenberg EBook, 2011 (Originally: James R. Osgood, McIlvaine & CO. 1893).

Micheal Clodfelter, *Warfare and Armed Conflicts: A Statistical Encyclopedia of Casualty and Other Figures, 1492-2015*, McFarland, 2017.

Christopher Clarck, *Iron Kingdom – Rise and Downfall of Prussia 1600-1947*, Penguin Books, 2007.

Martin Kitchen, *A History of Modern Germany, 1800–2000*, Blackwell Publishing, 2006.

John G. Gagliardo, *Germany under the Old Regime, 1600-1790*, Routledge, 2013.

Joachim Whaley, *Germany and the Holy Roman Empire Vol. 1 &2*, Oxford University Press, 2012.

Margaret Shennan, *The Rise of Brandenburg-Prussia*, Routledge, 1995.

Mary Fulbrook, *A Concise History of Germany*, Cambridge University Press, 1991.

S.A. Eddie, *Freedom's Price - Serfdom, Subjection, and Reform in Prussia, 1648-1848*, Oxford University Press, 2013.

Philip G. Dwyer, *The Rise of Prussia: Rethinking Prussian History, 1700-1830*, Routledge, 2013.

David Blackbourn, *The Long Nineteenth Century - A History of Germany, 1780-1914*, Oxford University Press, 1998.

Jason Philip Coy, *A Brief History of Germany*, Facts on File, 2011.

A, Farmer and A. Stiles, *The Unification of Germany 1815-1919*, Hodder Education, 2007.

Peter Wende, *A History of Germany*, Palgrave Macmillan, 2005.

Jonathan Steinberg, *Bismarck: A Life*, Oxford University Press, 2011.

Stefan Berger, *A Companion to Nineteenth-Century Europe 1789-1914*, Blackwell Publishing, 2006.

Dennis Showalter, *The Wars of German Unification*, Bloomsbury academic, 2015.

Otto Pflanze, *Bismarck and the Development of Germany - The Period of Unification 1815-1871*, Princeton University Press, 1963.

Donald S. Detwiler, *Germany - A Short History*, Southern Illinois University Press, 1989.

Ingram Content Group UK Ltd.
Milton Keynes UK
UKHW021032300323
419409UK00006B/386